# The Symposium

Xenophon

**Alpha Editions**

This edition published in 2024

ISBN : 9789366384818

Design and Setting By
**Alpha Editions**
www.alphaedis.com
Email - info@alphaedis.com

As per information held with us this book is in Public Domain.
This book is a reproduction of an important historical work. Alpha Editions uses the best technology to reproduce historical work in the same manner it was first published to preserve its original nature. Any marks or number seen are left intentionally to preserve its true form.

# THE SYMPOSIUM
## or
# The Banquet

I

For myself, (1) I hold to the opinion that not alone are the serious transactions of "good and noble men" (2) most memorable, but that words and deeds distinctive of their lighter moods may claim some record. (3) In proof of which contention, I will here describe a set of incidents within the scope of my experience. (4)

*(1) See Aristid. ii. foll.*

*(2) Or, "nature's noblemen."*

*(3) Cf. Plut. "Ages." 29 (Clough, iv. 35): "And indeed if, as Xenophon says, in conversation good men, even in their sports and at their wine, let fall many sayings that are worth preserving." See Grote, "Plato," ii. 228 foll. as to the sportive character of the work.*

*(4) Or, "let me describe a scene which I was witness of." See Hug. "Plat. Symp." p. xv. foll.*

The occasion was a horse-race (5) at the great Panathenaic festival. (6) Callias, (7) the son of Hipponicus, being a friend and lover of the boy Autolycus, (8) had brought the lad, himself the winner of the pankration, (9) to see the spectacle.

*(5) See "Hipparch," ii. 1.*

*(6) "Held towards the end of July (Hecatombaeon) every year, and with greater pomp every four years (the third of each Olympiad)."—Gow, 84, 129, n.*

*(7) Callias. Cobet, "Pros. X." p. 67 foll.; Boeckh, "P. E. A." p. 481.*

*(8) See Cobet, op. cit. p. 54; Plut. "Lysand." 15 (Clough, iii. 120); Grote, "H. G." ix. 261.*

*(9) 420 B.C., al. 421. The date is fixed by the "Autolycus" of Eupolis. See Athen. v. 216. For the pankration, which comprised wrestling and boxing, see Aristot. "Rhet." i. S. 14.*

As soon as the horse race was over, (10) Callias proceeded to escort Autolycus and his father, Lycon, to his house in the Piraeus, being attended also by Niceratus. (11) But catching sight of Socrates along with certain others (Critobulus, (12) Hermogenes, Antisthenes, and Charmides), he bade an attendant conduct the party with Autolycus, whilst he himself approached the group, exclaiming:

*(10) See A. Martin, op. cit. p. 265.*

*(11) Niceratus. See Cobet, op. cit. 71; Boeckh, "P. E. A." 480; Plat. "Lach." 200 C; "Hell." II. iii. 39; Lys. xviii.; Diod. xiv. 5.*

*(12) Critobulus, Hermogenes, Antisthenes, Charmides. See "Mem."*

A happy chance brings me across your path, just when I am about to entertain Autolycus and his father at a feast. The splendour of the entertainment shall be much enhanced, I need not tell you, if my hall (13) should happily be graced by worthies like yourselves, who have attained to purity of soul, (14) rather than by generals and cavalry commanders (15) and a crowd of place-hunters. (16)

*(13) Or, "dining-room." See Becker, "Charicles," 265.*

*(14) See Grote, "H. G." viii. 619 foll. Cf. Plat. "Rep." 527 D; "Soph." 230 E.*

*(15) Lit. Strategoi, Hipparchs.*

*(16) Or, "petitioners for offices of state." Reading {spoudarkhiais}.*

Whereat Socrates: When will you have done with your gibes, Callias? Why, because you have yourself spent sums of money on Protagoras, (17) and Gorgias, and Prodicus, and a host of others, to learn wisdom, must you pour contempt on us poor fellows, who are but self-taught tinkers (18) in philosophy compared with you?

*(17) As to Protagoras of Abdera, Gorgias of Leontini, Prodicus of Ceos, see Plat. "Prot." 314 C, "Rep." x. 600 C, "Apol." 19 E; "Anab." II. vi. 17; "Mem." II. i. 21; "Encyc. Brit." "Sophists," H. Jackson.*

*(18) Or, "hand-to-mouth cultivators of philosophy," "roturiers." Cf. Plat. "Rep." 565 A: "A third class who work for themselves"; Thuc. i. 141: "The Peloponnesians cultivate their own soil, and they have no wealth either public or private." Cf. "Econ." v. 4.*

Hitherto, no doubt (retorted Callias), although I had plenty of wise things to say, I have kept my wisdom to myself; but if only you will honour me with your company to-day, I promise to present myself in quite another light; you will see I am a person of no mean consideration after all. (19)

*(19) Or, "I will prove to you that I am worthy of infinite respect."*

Socrates and the others, while thanking Callias politely for the invitation, were not disposed at first to join the dinner party; but the annoyance of the other so to be put off was so obvious that in the end the party were persuaded to accompany their host.

After an interval devoted to gymnastic exercise (and subsequent anointing of the limbs) by some, whilst others of them took a bath, the guests were severally presented to the master of the house.

Autolycus was seated next his father, as was natural, (20) while the rest reclined on couches. Noting the scene presented, the first idea to strike the mind of any one must certainly have been that beauty has by nature something regal in it; and the more so, if it chance to be combined (as now in the person of Autolycus) with modesty and self-respect. Even as when a splendid object blazes forth at night, the eyes of men are riveted, (21) so now the beauty of Autolycus drew on him the gaze of all; nor was there one of those onlookers but was stirred to his soul's depth by him who sat there. (22) Some fell into unwonted silence, while the gestures of the rest were equally significant.

*(20) Al. "Autolycus found a seat beside his father, while the rest*

*reclined on couches in the usual fashion." See Schneider's note.*

*(21) Passage imitated by Max. Tyr. "Or." xxiv. 4.*

*(22) Cf. Plat. "Charm." 154.*

It seems the look betokening divine possession, no matter who the god, must ever be remarkable. Only, whilst the subject of each commoner emotion passion-whirled may be distinguished by flashings of the eye, by terror-striking tones of voice, and by the vehement fervour of the man's whole being, so he who is inspired by temperate and harmonious love (23) will wear a look of kindlier welcome in his eyes; the words he utters fall from his lips with softer intonation; and every gesture of his bodily frame conform to what is truly frank and liberal. Such, at any rate, the strange effects now wrought on Callias by love. He was like one transformed, the cynosure of all initiated in the mysteries of this divinity. (24)

*(23) Cf. Plat. "Rep." iii. 403 A: "Whereas true love is a love of*

*beauty and order, temperate and harmonious."*

*(24) Cf. "Econ." xxi. 12.*

So they supped in silence, the whole company, as if an injunction had been laid upon them by some superior power. But presently there came a knocking on the door! Philippus the jester bade the doorkeeper (25) announce him, with apologies for seeking a night's lodging: (26) he had come, he said, provided with all necessaries for dining, at a friend's expense: his attendant was much galled with carrying, nothing but an empty breadbasket. (27) To this announcement Callias, appealing to his guests, replied: "It would never do to begrudge the shelter of one's roof: (28) let him come in." And as he spoke, he glanced across to where Autolycus was seated, as if to say: "I wonder how you take the jest."

*(25) Lit. "him who answers the knock," "the concierge" or hall-porter.*

*Cf. Theophr. "Char." xiv. 7; Aristot. "Oec." i. 6.*

*(26) Lit. "and why he wished to put up."*

*(27) Lit. "and being breakfastless"; cf. Theocr. i. 51. The jester's humour resembles Pistol's ("Merry Wives," i. 3. 23) "O base Hungarian wight!"*

*(28) Or, "How say you, my friends, it would hardly do, methinks, to shut the door upon him." See Becker, "Charicles," p. 92.*

Meanwhile the jester, standing at the door of the apartment where the feast was spread, addressed the company:

I believe you know, sirs, that being a jester by profession, it is my business to make jokes. I am all the readier, therefore, to present myself, feeling convinced it is a better joke to come to dinner thus unbidden than by solemn invitation.

Be seated, (29) then (replied the host). The company are fully fed on serious thoughts, you see, if somewhat starved of food for laughter.

*(29) Lit. "Pray, find a couch then."*

The feast proceeded; and, if only to discharge the duty laid upon him at a dinner-party, Philippus must try at once to perpetrate a jest. Failing to stir a smile, poor fellow, he made no secret of his perturbation. Presently he tried again; and for the second time the joke fell flat. Whereat he paused abruptly in the middle of the course, and muffling up his face, fell prostrate on the couch.

Then Callias: What ails you, sirrah? Have you the cramp? the toothache? what?

To which the other heaving a deep groan: Yes, Callias, an atrocious ache; since laughter has died out among mankind, my whole estate is bankrupt. (30) In old days I would be asked to dinner to amuse the company with jests. (31) Now all is changed, and who will be at pains to ask me out to dinner any more? I might as well pretend to be immortal as to be serious. Nor will any one invite me in hopes of reclining at my board in his turn. Everyone knows so serious a thing as dinner in my house was never heard of; it's against the rules—the more's the pity.

*(30) Cf. "Cyrop." VI. i. 3; Plat. "Laws," 677 C.*

*(31) Lit. "by the laughter which I stirred in them."*

And as he spoke he blew his nose and snuffled, uttering the while so truly dolorous a moan (32) that everybody fell to soothing him. "They would all laugh again another day," they said, and so implored him to have done and eat his dinner; till Critobulus could not stand his lamentation longer, but broke into a peal of laughter. The welcome sound sufficed. The sufferer unveiled his face, and thus addressed his inner self: (33) "Be of good cheer, my soul, there are many battles (34) yet in store for us," and so he fell to discussing the viands once again.

*(32) Philippus would seem to have anticipated Mr. Woodward; see*

*Prologue to "She Stoops to Conquer":*

Pray, would you know the reason I'm crying? The Comic Muse long sick is now a-dying! And if she goes...

*(33) Cf. "Cyrop." I. iv. 13; Eur. "Med." 1056, 1242; Aristoph. "Ach." 357, 480.*

*(34) Or add, "ere we have expended our last shot." Philippus puns on*

*the double sense of {sumbolai}. Cf. Aristoph. "Ach." 1210, where*

*Lamachus groans {talas ego xumboles bareias}, and Dicaeopolis*

*replies {tois Khousi gar tis xumbolas epratteto}.*

Lam. 'Twas at the final charge; I'd paid before

A number of the rogues; at least a score.

Dic. It was a most expensive charge you bore:

Poor Lamachus! he was forced to pay the score.

H. Frere.

II

Now the tables were removed, and in due order they had poured out the libation, and had sung the hymn. (1) To promote the revelry, there entered now a Syracusan, with a trio of assistants: the first, a flute-girl, perfect in her art; and next, a dancing-girl, skilled to perform all kinds of wonders; lastly, in the bloom of beauty, a boy, who played the harp and danced with infinite grace. This Syracusan went about exhibiting his troupe, whose wonderful performance was a source of income to him.

*(1) See Plat. "Symp." 176 A; Athen. ix. 408.*

After the girl had played to them upon the flute, and then the boy in turn upon the harp, and both performers, as it would appear, had set the hearts of every one rejoicing, Socrates turned to Callias:

A feast, upon my word, O princeliest entertainer! (2) Was it not enough to set before your guests a faultless dinner, but you must feast our eyes and ears on sights and sounds the most delicious?

*(2) Lit. "in consummate style."*

To which the host: And that reminds me, a supply of unguents might not be amiss; (3) what say you? Shall we feast on perfumes also? (4)

*(3) Lit. "suppose I tell the servant to bring in some perfumes, so that we may further feast on fragrance..." Cf. Theophr. "Char." vii. 6 (Jebb ad loc.)*

*(4) See Athen. xv. 686.*

No, I protest (the other answered). Scents resemble clothes. One dress is beautiful on man and one on woman; and so with fragrance: what becomes the woman, ill becomes the man. Did ever man anoint himself with oil of myrrh to please his fellow? Women, and especially young women (like our two friends' brides, Niceratus' and Critobulus'), need no perfume, being but compounds themselves of fragrance. (5) No, sweeter than any perfume else to women is good olive-oil, suggestive of the training-school: (6) sweet if present, and when absent longed for. And why? Distinctions vanish with the use of perfumes. The freeman and the slave have forthwith both alike one odour. But the scents derived from toils—those toils which every free man loves (7)—need customary habit first, and time's distillery, if they are to be sweet with freedom's breath, at last. (8)

*(5) Cf. Solomon's Song, iv. 10: "How fair is thy love, my sister, my spouse! how much better is thy love than wine! and the smell of thine ointments than all spices!"*

*(6) Lit. "the gymnasium."*

*(7) Cf. Aristoph. "Clouds," 1002 foll. See J. A. Symonds, "The Greek*

*Poets," 1st s., p. 281.*

*(8) See "Mem." III. x. 5; "Cyrop." VIII. i. 43.*

Here Lycon interposed: That may be well enough for youths, but what shall we do whose gymnastic days are over? What fragrance is left for us?

Soc. Why, that of true nobility, of course.

Lyc. And whence shall a man obtain this chrism?

Soc. Not from those that sell perfumes and unguents, in good sooth.

Lyc. But whence, then?

Soc. Theognis has told us:

*From the good thou shalt learn good things, but if with the evil*

*Thou holdest converse, thou shalt lose the wit that is in thee. (9)*

*(9) Theog. 35 foll. See "Mem." I. ii. 20; Plat. "Men." 95 D.*

Lyc. (turning to his son). Do you hear that, my son?

That he does (Socrates answered for the boy), and he puts the precept into practice also; to judge, at any rate, from his behaviour. When he had set his heart on carrying off the palm of victory in the pankration, he took you into his counsel; (10) and will again take counsel to discover the fittest friend to aid him in his high endeavour, (11) and with this friend associate.

*(10) It looks as if something had been lost intimating that Autolycus*

*would have need of some one to instruct him in spiritual things.*

*For attempts to fill up the lacuna see Schenkl.*

*(11) Or, "these high pursuits."*

Thereupon several of the company exclaimed at once. "Where will he find a teacher to instruct him in that wisdom?" one inquired. "Why, it is not to be taught!" exclaimed another; to which a third rejoined: "Why should it not be learnt as well as other things?" (12)

*(12) Cf. for the question {ei arete didakton}, "Mem." I. ii. 19; IV.*

*i; "Cyrop." III. i. 17; III. iii. 53.*

Then Socrates: The question would seem at any rate to be debatable. Suppose we defer it till another time, and for the present not interrupt the programme of proceedings. I see, the dancing-girl is standing ready; they are handing her some hoops.

And at the instant her fellow with the flute commenced a tune to keep her company, whilst some one posted at her side kept handing her the hoops till she had twelve in all. With these in her hands she fell to dancing, and the while she danced she flung the hoops into the air—overhead she sent them twirling—judging the height they must be thrown to catch them, as they fell, in perfect time. (13)

(13) *"In time with the music and the measure of the dance."*

Then Socrates: The girl's performance is one proof among a host of others, sirs, that woman's nature is nowise inferior to man's. All she wants is strength and judgment; (14) and that should be an encouragement to those of you who have wives, to teach them whatever you would have them know as your associates. (15)

(14) Reading, as vulg. {gnomes de kai iskhuos deitai}; al. continuing {ouden} from the first half of the sentence, transl. *"she has no lack of either judgment or physical strength."* Lange conj. {romes} for {gnomes}, *"all she needs is force and strength of body."* See Newman, op. cit. i. 419.

(15) Lit. *"so that, if any of you has a wife, he may well take heart and teach her whatever he would wish her to know in dealing with her."* Cf. *"N. A." i. 17.*

Antisthenes rejoined: If that is your conclusion, Socrates, why do you not tutor your own wife, Xanthippe, (16) instead of letting her (17) remain, of all the wives that are, indeed that ever will be, I imagine, the most shrewish?

(16) See Cobet, *"Pros. Xen." p. 56;* *"Mem." II. ii. 1; Aul. Gell. "N. A." i. 17.*

(17) Lit. *"dealing with her," "finding in her";* {khro} corresponding to {khresthai} in Socrates' remarks.

Well now, I will tell you (he answered). I follow the example of the rider who wishes to become an expert horseman: "None of your soft-mouthed, docile animals for me," he says; "the horse for me to own must show some spirit": (18) in the belief, no doubt, if he can manage such an animal, it will be easy enough to deal with every other horse besides. And that is just my case. I wish to deal with human beings, to associate with man in general; hence my choice of wife. (19) I know full well, if I can tolerate her spirit, I can with ease attach myself to every human being else.

*(18) Lit. "Because I see the man who aims at skill in horsemanship does not care to own a soft-mouthed, docile animal, but some restive, fiery creature."*

*(19) Lit. "being anxious to have intercourse with all mankind, to deal with every sort of human being, I possess my wife."*

A well-aimed argument, not wide of the mark by any means! (20) the company were thinking.

*(20) Cf. Plat. "Theaet." 179 C.*

Hereupon a large hoop studded with a bristling row of upright swords (21) was introduced; and into the centre of this ring of knives and out of it again the girl threw somersaults backwards, forwards, several times, till the spectators were in terror of some accident; but with the utmost coolness and without mishap the girl completed her performance.

*(21) See Becker, "Char." p. 101. Cf. Plat. "Symp." 190; "Euthyd." 294.*

Here Socrates, appealing to Antisthenes: None of the present company, I take it, who have watched this spectacle will ever again deny that courage can be taught, (22) when the girl there, woman should she be, rushes so boldly into the midst of swords.

*(22) Cf. "Mem." III. ix. 1.*

He, thus challenged, answered: No; and what our friend, the Syracusan here, should do is to exhibit his dancing-girl to the state. (23) Let him tell the authorities he is prepared, for a consideration, to give the whole Athenian people courage to face the hostile lances at close quarters.

*(23) Or, "to the city," i.e. of Athens.*

Whereat the jester: An excellent idea, upon my word; and when it happens, may I be there to see that mighty orator (24) Peisander learning to throw somersaults (25) into swords; since incapacity to look a row of lances in the face at present makes him shy of military service. (26)

*(24) Or, "tribune of the people." Cf. Plat. "Gorg." 520 B; "Laws," 908 D.*

*(25) Or, "learning to go head over heels into swords."*

*(26) For Peisander see Cobet, "Pros. Xen." p. 46 foll. A thoroughgoing oligarch (Thuc. viii. 90), he was the occasion of much mirth to the comic writers (so Grote, "H. G." viii. 12). See re his "want of spirit" Aristoph. "Birds," 1556:*

{entha kai Peisandros elthe deomenos psukhen idein, e zont ekeinon proulipe, k.t.l.}

*where the poet has a fling at Socrates also:*

Socrates beside the brink, Summons from the murky sink Many a disembodied ghost; And Peisander reached the coast To raise the spirit that he lost; With conviction strange and new, A gawky camel which he slew, Like Ulysses.—Whereupon, etc.

H. Frere

*Cf. "Peace," 395; "Lysistr." 490.*

At this stage of the proceedings the boy danced.

The dance being over, Socrates exclaimed: Pray, did you notice how the beauty of the child, so lovely in repose, became enhanced with every movement of his supple body?

To which Charmides replied: How like a flatterer you are! one would think you had set yourself to puff the dancing-master. (27)

*(27) See "The Critic," I. ii.*

To be sure (he answered solemnly); and there's another point I could not help observing: how while he danced no portion of his body remained idle; neck and legs and hands together, one and all were exercised. (28) That is how a man should dance, who wants to keep his body light and healthy. (29) (Then turning to the Syracusan, he added): I cannot say how much obliged I should be to you, O man of Syracuse, for lessons in deportment. Pray teach me my steps. (30)

*(28) Cf. "Pol. Lac." v. 9.*

*(29) Cf. Aristot. "H. A." vi. 21. 4.*

*(30) "Gestures," "postures," "figures." See Eur. "Cycl." 221; Aristoph. "Peace," 323; Isocr. "Antid." 183.*

And what use will you make of them? (the other asked).

God bless me! I shall dance, of course (he answered).

The remark was greeted with a peal of merriment.

Then Socrates, with a most serious expression of countenance: (31) You are pleased to laugh at me. Pray, do you find it so ridiculous my wishing to improve my health by exercise? or to enjoy my victuals better? to sleep better? or is it the sort of exercise I set my heart on? Not like those runners of the long race, (32) to have my legs grow muscular and my shoulders leaner in proportion; nor like a boxer, thickening chest and shoulders at expense of legs; but by distribution of the toil throughout my limbs (33) I seek to give an even balance to my body. Or are you laughing to think that I shall not in future have to seek a partner in the training school, (34) whereby it will not be necessary for an old man like myself to strip in public? (35) All I shall need will be a seven-sofa'd chamber, (36) where I can warm to work, (37) just like the lad here who has found this room quite ample for the purpose. And in winter I shall do gymnastics (38) under cover, or when the weather is broiling under shade.... But what is it you keep on laughing at—the wish on my part to reduce to moderate size a paunch a trifle too rotund? Is that the source of merriment? (39) Perhaps you are not aware, my friends, that Charmides—yes! he there—caught me only the other morning in the act of dancing?

*(31) "Bearing a weighty and serious brow."*

*(32) "Like your runner of the mile race." Cf. Plat. "Prot." 335 E.*

*(33) Or, "resolute exercise of the whole body." See Aristot. "Pol." viii. 4. 9; "Rhet." i. 5. 14.*

*(34) Or, "be dependent on a fellow-gymnast." "Pol. Lac." ix. 5; Plat.*

*"Soph."* 218 B; *"Laws,"* 830 B; *"Symp."* 217 B, C.

(35) Or, "to strip in public when my hair turns gray." Socrates was (421 B.C.) about 50, but is pictured, I think, as an oldish man.

(36) See Aristot. *"H. A."* ix. 45. 1; *"Econ."* viii. 13.

(37) Passage referred to by Diog. Laert. ii. 5. 15; Lucian, *"de Salt."* 25; Plut. *"Praec. San."* 496.

(38) "Take my exercise."

(39) Zeune cf. Max. Tyr. *"Diss."* vii. 9; xxxix. 5.

Yes, that I will swear to (the other answered), and at first I stood aghast, I feared me you had parted with your senses; but when I heard your explanation, pretty much what you have just now told us, I went home and—I will not say, began to dance myself (it is an accomplishment I have not been taught as yet), but I fell to sparring, (40) an art of which I have a very pretty knowledge.

(40) *"Sparring,"* etc., an art which Quintil. *"Inst. Or."* i. 11, 17, attributes to Socrates. Cf. Herod. vi. 129 concerning Hippocleides; and Rich, *"Dict. of Antiq."* s.v. *"Chironomia."*

That's true, upon my life! (exclaimed the jester). One needs but look at you to see there's not a dram of difference between legs and shoulders. (41) I'll be bound, if both were weighed in the scales apart, like "tops and bottoms," the clerks of the market (42) would let you off scot-free.

(41) Lit. *"your legs are equal in weight with your shoulders."* Cf. *"Od."* xviii. 373, {elikes... isophoroi boes}, *"of equal age and force to bear the yoke."*—Butcher and Lang.

(42) See Boeckh, *"Public Economy of Athens,"* p. 48; Aristoph. *"Acharn."* 723; Lys. 165, 34.

Then Callias: O Socrates, do please invite me when you begin your dancing lessons. I will be your vis-a-vis, (43) and take lessons with you.

*(43) Cf. "Anab." V. iv. 12.*

Come on (the jester shouted), give us a tune upon the pipe, and let me show you how to dance.

So saying up he got, and mimicked the dances of the boy and girl in burlesque fashion, and inasmuch as the spectators had been pleased to think the natural beauty of the boy enhanced by every gesture of his body in the dance, so the jester must give a counter-representation, (44) in which each twist and movement of his body was a comical exaggeration of nature.

*(44) Reading {antepedeizen}. Cf. Plat. "Theaet." 162 B; "Ages." i. 12;*

*if vulg. {antapedeizen}, transl. "would prove per contra each*

*bend," etc. Cf. Aristot. "Rhet." ii. 26. 3.*

And since the girl had bent herself backwards and backwards, till she was nearly doubled into the form of a hoop, so he must try to imitate a hoop by stooping forwards and ducking down his head.

And as finally, the boy had won a round of plaudits for the manner in which he kept each muscle of the body in full exercise whilst dancing, so now the jester, bidding the flute-girl quicken the time (presto! presto! prestissimo!), fell to capering madly, tossing legs and arms and head together, until he was fairly tired out, and threw himself dead beat upon the sofa, gasping:

There, that's a proof that my jigs too are splendid exercise; at any rate, I am dying of thirst; let the attendant kindly fill me the mighty goblet. (45)

*(45) Cf. Plat. "Symp." 223 C.*

Quite right (said Callias), and we will pledge you. Our throats are parched with laughing at you.

At this point Socrates: Nay, gentlemen, if drinking is the order of the day, I heartily approve. Wine it is in very truth that moistens the soul of man, (46) that lulls at once all cares to sleep, even as mandragora (47) drugs our human senses, and at the same time kindles light-hearted thoughts, (48) as oil a flame. Yet it fares with the banquets of men, (49) if I mistake not, precisely as with plants that spring and shoot on earth. When God gives these vegetable growths too full a draught of rain, they cannot lift their heads nor feel the light air breathe through them; but if they drink in only the glad supply they need, they stand erect, they shoot apace, and reach maturity of fruitage. So we, too, if we drench our throats with over-copious draughts, (50) ere long may find our legs begin to reel and our thoughts begin to falter; (51) we shall scarce be able to draw breath, much less to speak a word in season. But if (to borrow language from the mint of Gorgias (52)), if only the attendants will bedew us with a frequent mizzle (53) of small glasses, we shall not be violently driven on by wine to drunkenness, but with sweet seduction reach the goal of sportive levity.

(46) Cf. Plat. "Laws," 649; Aristoph. "Knights," 96:

Come, quick now, bring me a lusty stoup of wine, To moisten my understanding and inspire me (H. Frere).

(47) Cf. Plat. "Rep." vi. 488 C; Dem. "Phil." iv. 133. 1; Lucian v.,

"Tim." 2; lxxiii., "Dem. Enc." 36. See "Othello," iii. 3. 330:

Not poppy, nor mandragora, Nor all the drowsy syrups of the world;

"Antony and Cl." i. 5, 4.

(48) Cf. 1 Esdras iii. 20: "It turneth also every thought into jollity

and mirth," {eis euokhian kai euphrosunen}. The whole passage is

quoted by Athen. 504. Stob. "Fl." lvi. 17.

(49) Reading {sumposia}, cf. Theog. 298, 496; or if after Athen.

{somata} transl. "persons."

(50) Or, "if we swallow at a gulp the liquor." Cf. Plat. "Sym." 176 D.

(51) See "Cyrop." I. iii. 10, VIII. viii. 10; Aristoph. "Wasps," 1324;

"Pol. Lac." v. 7.

(52) For phrases filed by Gorgias, see Aristot. "Rhet." iii. 3;

"faults of taste in the use of metaphors," Longin. "de Subl." 3.

See also Plat. "Symp." 198 C.

(53) Cf. Aristoph. "Peace," 1141; Theophr. "Lap." 13; Lucian, xvii.,

"De merc. cond." 27; Cic. "Cat. m." 14, transl. "pocula... minuta atque rorantia."

The proposition was unanimously carried, with a rider appended by Philippus: The cup-bearers should imitate good charioteers, and push the cups round, quickening the pace each circuit. (54)

*(54) Or, "at something faster than a hand-gallop each round." See the drinking song in "Antony and Cl." i. 7. 120.*

III

During this interval, whilst the cup-bearers carried out their duties, the boy played on the lyre tuned to accompany the flute, and sang. (1)

*(1) Cf. Plat. "Laws," 812 C; Aristot. "Poet." i. 4.*

The performance won the plaudits of the company, and drew from Charmides a speech as follows: Sirs, what Socrates was claiming in behalf of wine applies in my opinion no less aptly to the present composition. So rare a blending of boyish and of girlish beauty, and of voice with instrument, is potent to lull sorrow to sleep, and to kindle Aphrodite's flame.

Then Socrates, reverting in a manner to the charge: The young people have fully proved their power to give us pleasure. Yet, charming as they are, we still regard ourselves, no doubt, as much their betters. What a shame to think that we should here be met together, and yet make no effort ourselves to heighten the festivity! (2)

*(2) See Plat. "Prot." 347 D; "A company like this of ours, and men such as we profess to be, do not require the help of another's voice," etc.—Jowett. Cf. id. "Symp." 176: "To-day let us have conversation instead; and if you will allow me, I will tell you what sort of conversation."*

Several of the company exclaimed at once: Be our director then yourself. Explain what style of talk we should engage in to achieve that object. (3)

*(3) {exegou}. "Prescribe the form of words we must lay hold of to achieve the object, and we will set to work, arch-casuist."*

Nothing (he replied) would please me better than to demand of Callias a prompt performance of his promise. He told us, you recollect, if we would dine with him, he would give us an exhibition of his wisdom.

To which challenge Callias: That I will readily, but you on your side, one and all, must propound some virtue of which you claim to have the knowledge.

Socrates replied: At any rate, not one of us will have the least objection to declaring what particular thing he claims to know as best worth having.

Agreed (proceeded Callias); and for my part I proclaim at once what I am proudest of. My firm belief is, I have got the gift to make my fellow-mortals better.

Make men better! (cried Antisthenes); and pray how? by teaching them some base mechanic art? or teaching them nobility of soul? (4)

*(4) Or, "beauty and nobility of soul" ({kalokagathia}). See "Mem." I. vi. 14.*

The latter (he replied), if justice (5) be synonymous with that high type of virtue.

*(5) i.e. "social uprightness."*

Of course it is (rejoined Antisthenes) the most indisputable specimen. Since, look you, courage and wisdom may at times be found calamitous to friends or country, (6) but justice has no single point in common with injustice, right and wrong cannot commingle. (7)

*(6) See "Mem." IV. ii. 33.*

*(7) i.e. "the one excludes the other."*

Well then (proceeded Callias), as soon (8) as every one has stated his peculiar merit, (9) I will make no bones of letting you into my secret. You shall learn the art by which I consummate my noble end. (10) So now, Niceratus, suppose you tell us on what knowledge you most pride yourself.

*(8) Reading {emon}. Al. {umon}, "when you others."*

*(9) Lit. "what he has for which to claim utility."*

*(10) Or, "give the work completeness." Cf. Plat. "Charm." 173 A; "Gorg." 454 A.*

He answered: My father, (11) in his pains to make me a good man, compelled me to learn the whole of Homer's poems, and it so happens that even now I can repeat the "Iliad" and the "Odyssey" by heart. (12)

*(11) Nicias.*

*(12) Of, "off-hand." See "Mem." III. vi. 9; Plat. "Theaet." 142 D.*

You have not forgotten (interposed Antisthenes), perhaps, that besides yourself there is not a rhapsodist who does not know these epics?

Forgotten! is it likely (he replied), considering I had to listen to them almost daily?

Ant. And did you ever come across a sillier tribe of people than these same rhapsodists? (13)

*(13) Cf. "Mem." IV. ii. 10.*

Nic. Not I, indeed. Don't ask me to defend their wits.

It is plain (suggested Socrates), they do not know the underlying meaning. (14) But you, Niceratus, have paid large sums of money to Anaximander, and Stesimbrotus, and many others, (15) so that no single point in all that costly lore is lost upon you. (16) But what (he added, turning to Critobulus) do you most pride yourself upon?

*(14) i.e. "they haven't the key (of knowledge) to the allegorical or*

*spiritual meaning of the sacred text." Cf. Plat. "Crat." 407;*

*"Ion," 534; "Rep." 378, 387; "Theaet." 180; "Prot." 316. See*

*Grote, "H. G." i. 564.*

*(15) See Aristot. "Rhet." iii. 11, 13. "Or we may describe Niceratus*

*(not improbably our friend) as a 'Philoctetes stung by Pratys,'*

*using the simile of Thrasymachus when he saw Niceratus after his*

*defeat by Pratys in the rhapsody with his hair still dishevelled*

*and his face unwashed."—Welldon. As to Stesimbrotus, see Plat.*

*"Ion," 530: "Ion. Very true, Socrates; interpretation has*

*certainly been the most laborious part of my art; and I believe*

*myself able to speak about Homer better than any man; and that neither Metrodorus of Lampsacus, nor Stesimbrotus of Thasos, nor Glaucon, nor any one else who ever was, had as good ideas about Homer, or as many of them, as I have."—Jowett. Anaximander, probably of Lampsacus, the author of a {'Erologia}; see Cobet, "Pros. Xen." p. 8.*

*(16) Or, "you will not have forgotten one point of all that precious teaching." Like Sir John Falstaff's page (2 "Henry IV." ii. 2. 100), Niceratus, no doubt, has got many "a crown's worth of good interpretations."*

On beauty (answered Critobulus).

What (Socrates rejoined), shall you be able to maintain that by your beauty you can make us better?

Crit. That will I, or prove myself a shabby sort of person.

Soc. Well, and what is it you pride yourself upon, Antisthenes?

On wealth (he answered).

Whereupon Hermogenes inquired: Had he then a large amount of money? (17)

*(17) i.e. "out at interest," or, "in the funds," as we should say.*

Not one sixpence: (18) that I swear to you (he answered).

*(18) Lit. "not an obol" = "a threepenny bit," circa.*

Herm. Then you possess large property in land?

Ant. Enough, I daresay, for the youngster there, Autolycus, to dust himself withal. (19)

*(19) i.e. "to sprinkle himself with sand, after anointing." Cf. Lucian, xxxviii., "Amor." 45.*

Well, we will lend you our ears, when your turn comes (exclaimed the others).

Soc. And do you now tell us, Charmides, on what you pride yourself.

Oh, I, for my part, pride myself on poverty (he answered).

Upon my word, a charming business! (exclaimed Socrates). Poverty! of all things the least liable to envy; seldom, if ever, an object of contention; (20) never guarded, yet always safe; the more you starve it, the stronger it grows.

*(20) Cf. Plat. "Rep." 521 A; "Laws," 678 C.*

And you, Socrates, yourself (their host demanded), what is it you pride yourself upon?

Then he, with knitted brows, quite solemnly: On pandering. (21) And when they laughed to hear him say this, (22) he continued: Laugh to your hearts content, my friends; but I am certain I could make a fortune, if I chose to practise this same art.

*(21) Or, more politely, "on playing the go-between." See Grote, "H.*

*G." viii. 457, on the "extremely Aristophanic" character of the*

*"Symposium" of Xenophon.*

*(22) "Him, the master, thus declare himself."*

At this point Lycon, turning to Philippus: We need not ask you what you take the chiefest pride in. What can it be, you laughter-making man, except to set folk laughing?

Yes (he answered), and with better right, I fancy, than Callippides, (23) the actor, who struts and gives himself such pompous airs, to think that he alone can set the crowds a-weeping in the theatre. (24)

*(23) For illustrative tales about him see Plut. "Ages." xxi.; "Alcib."*

*xxxii.; Polyaen. vi. 10. Cf. "Hell." IV. viii. 16.*

*(24) Or, "set for their sins a-weeping."*

And now you, Lycon, tell us, won't you (asked Antisthenes), what it is you take the greatest pride in?

You all of you, I fancy, know already what that is (the father answered); it is in my son here.

And the lad himself (some one suggested) doubtless prides himself, beyond all else, on having won the prize of victory.

At that Autolycus (and as he spoke he blushed) answered for himself: (25) No indeed, not I.

*(25) Cf. Plat. "Charm." 158 C.*

The company were charmed to hear him speak, and turned and looked; and some one asked: On what is it then, Autolycus?

To which he answered: On my father (and leaned closer towards him).

At which sight Callias, turning to the father: Do you know you are the richest man in the whole world, Lycon?

To which Lycon: Really, I was not aware of that before.

Then Callias: Why then, it has escaped you that you would refuse the whole of Persia's wealth, (26) in exchange for your own son.

*(26) Lit. "of the Great King." Cf. "Cyrop." VIII. iii. 26.*

Most true (he answered), I plead guilty; here and now I am convicted (27) of being the wealthiest man in all the world!

*(27) "Caught flagrante delicto. I do admit I do out-Croesus Croesus."*

And you, Hermogenes, on what do you plume yourself most highly? (asked Niceratus).

On the virtue and the power of my friends (he answered), and that being what they are, they care for me.

At this remark they turned their eyes upon the speaker, and several spoke together, asking: Will you make them known to us?

I shall be very happy (he replied).

IV

At this point, Socrates took up the conversation: It now devolves on us to prove in turn that what we each have undertaken to defend is really valuable.

Then Callias: Be pleased to listen to me first: My case is this, that while the rest of you go on debating what justice and uprightness are, (1) I spend my time in making men more just and upright.

*(1) {to to dikaion}; cf. "Mem." IV. iv.*

Soc. And how do you do that, good sir?

Call. By giving money, to be sure.

Antisthenes sprang to his feet at once, and with the manner of a cross-examiner demanded: Do human beings seem to you to harbour justice in their souls, or in their purses, (2) Callias?

*(2) Or, "pockets."*

Call. In their souls.

Ant. And do you pretend to make their souls more righteous by putting money in their pockets?

Call. Undoubtedly.

Ant. Pray how?

Call. In this way. When they know that they are furnished with the means, that is to say, my money, to buy necessaries, they would rather not incur the risk of evil-doing, and why should they?

Ant. And pray, do they repay you these same moneys?

Call. I cannot say they do.

Ant. Well then, do they requite your gifts of gold with gratitude?

Call. No, not so much as a bare "Thank you." In fact, some of them are even worse disposed towards me when they have got my money than before.

Now, here's a marvel! (exclaimed Antisthenes, and as he spoke he eyed the witness with an air of triumph). You can render people just to all the world, but towards yourself you cannot?

Pray, where's the wonder? (asked the other). Do you not see what scores of carpenters and house-builders there are who spend their time in building houses for half the world; but for themselves they simply cannot do it, and are forced to live in lodgings. And so admit that home-thrust, Master Sophist; (3) and confess yourself confuted.

*(3) "Professor of wisdom."*

Upon my soul, he had best accept his fate (4) (said Socrates). Why, after all, you are only like those prophets who proverbially foretell the future for mankind, but cannot foresee what is coming upon themselves.

*(4) Or, "the coup de grace."*

And so the first discussion ended. (5)

*(5) Or, "so ended fytte the first of the word-controversy."*

Thereupon Niceratus: Lend me your ears, and I will tell you in what respects you shall be better for consorting with myself. I presume, without my telling you, you know that Homer, being the wisest of mankind, has touched upon nearly every human topic in his poems. (6) Whosoever among you, therefore, would fain be skilled in economy, or oratory, or

- 22 -

strategy; whose ambition it is to be like Achilles, or Ajax, Nestor, or Odysseus—one and all pay court to me, for I have all this knowledge at my fingers' ends.

*(6) Or, "his creations are all but coextensive with every mortal*

*thing."*

Pray (interposed Antisthenes), (7) do you also know the way to be a king? (8) since Homer praises Agamemnon, you are well aware, as being

*A goodly king and eke a spearman bold. (9)*

*(7) Some modern critics (e.g. F. Dummler, "Antisthenica," p. 29 foll.)*

*maintain plausibly that the author is here glancing (as also Plato*

*in the "Ion") at Antisthenes' own treatises against the*

*Rhapsodists and on a more correct interpretation of Homer, {peri*

*exegeton} and {peri 'Omerou}.*

*(8) Or, "Have you the knowledge also how to play the king?"*

*(9) "Il." iii. 179. See "Mem." III. ii. 2.*

Nic. Full well I know it, and full well I know the duty of a skilful charioteer; how he who holds the ribbons must turn his chariot nigh the pillar's edge (10)

Himself inclined upon the polished chariot-board A little to the left of the twin pair: the right hand horse Touch with the prick, and shout a cheery shout, and give him rein. (11)

I know another thing besides, and you may put it to the test this instant, if you like. Homer somewhere has said: (12)

*And at his side an onion, which to drink gives relish.*

So if some one will but bring an onion, you shall reap the benefit of my sage lore (13) in less than no time, and your wine will taste the sweeter.

*(10) "Il." xxiii. 335; Plat. "Ion," 537.*

*(11) Lit. "yield him the reins with his hands."*

*(12)* *"Il." xi.630: "And set out a leek savourer of drink" (Purves).*

*Plat. "Ion," 538 C.*

*(13) "My culinary skill."*

Here Charmides exclaimed: Good sirs, let me explain. Niceratus is anxious to go home, redolent of onions, so that his fair lady may persuade herself, it never entered into anybody's head to kiss her lord. (14)

*(14) See Shakesp. "Much Ado," v. 2. 51 foll.; "Mids. N. D." iv. 2.*

Bless me, that isn't all (continued Socrates); if we do not take care, we shall win ourselves a comic reputation. (15) A relish must it be, in very truth, that can sweeten cup as well as platter, this same onion; and if we are to take to munching onions for desert, see if somebody does not say of us, "They went to dine with Callias, and got more than their deserts, the epicures." (16)

*(15) Lit. "I warrant you! (quoth Socrates) and there's another funny*

*notion we have every chance of getting fathered on us."*

*(16) Or, "and had a most hilarious and herbaceous time."*

No fear of that (rejoined Niceratus). Always take a bite of onion before speeding forth to battle, just as your patrons of the cock-pit give their birds a feed of garlic (17) before they put them for the fight. But for ourselves our thoughts are less intent perhaps on dealing blows than blowing kisses. (18)

*(17) Cf. Aristoph. "Knights," 494:*

Chorus. And here's the garlic. Swallow it down! Sausage Seller.... What for? Chorus. It will prime you up and make you fight the better.

H. Frere.

*(18) "We are concerned less with the lists of battle than of love";*

*"we meditate no furious close of battle but of lips." Lit. "how we*

*shall kiss some one rather than do battle with."*

After such sort the theme of their discourse reached its conclusion.

Then Critobulus spoke: It is now my turn, I think, to state to you the grounds on which I pride myself on beauty. (19)

*(19) See "Hellenica Essays," p. 353.*

A chorus of voices rejoined: Say on.

Crit. To begin with, if I am not beautiful, as methinks I be, you will bring on your own heads the penalty of perjury; for, without waiting to have the oath administered, you are always taking the gods to witness that you find me beautiful. And I must needs believe you, for are you not all honourable men? (20) If I then be so beautiful and affect you, even as I also am affected by him whose fair face here attracts me, (21) I swear by all the company of heaven I would not choose the great king's empire in exchange for what I am—the beauty of the world, the paragon of animals. (22) And at this instant I feast my eyes on Cleinias (23) gladlier than on all other sights which men deem fair. Joyfully will I welcome blindness to all else, if but these eyes may still behold him and him only. With sleep and night I am sore vexed, which rob me of his sight; but to daylight and the sun I owe eternal thanks, for they restore him to me, my heart's joy, Cleinias. (24)

*(20) Or, "beautiful and good."*

*(21) Or, "whose fair face draws me." Was Cleinias there as a "muta persona"? Hardly, in spite of {nun}. It is the image of him which is present to the mind's eye.*

*(22) Lit. "being beautiful"; but there is a touch of bombast infused into the speech by the artist. Cf. the speech of Callias ("Hell." VI. iii. 3) and, for the humour, "Cyrop." passim.*

*(23) See Cobet, "Pros. Xen." p. 59. Cf. "Mem." I. iii. 8.*

*(24) Or, "for that they reveal his splendour to me."*

Yes, and herein also have we, the beautiful, (25) just claim to boast. The strong man may by dint of toil obtain good things; the brave, by danger boldly faced, and the wise by eloquence of speech; but to the beautiful alone it is given to achieve all ends in absolute quiescence. To take myself as an example. I know that riches are a sweet possession, yet sweeter far to me to give all that I have to Cleinias than to receive a fortune from another. Gladly would I become a slave—ay, forfeit freedom—if Cleinias would deign to be my lord. Toil in his service were easier for me than rest from labour: danger incurred in his behalf far sweeter than security of days. So that if you, Callias, may boast of making men more just and upright, to me belongs by juster right than yours to train mankind to every excellence. We are the true inspirers (26) who infuse some subtle fire into amorous souls, we beauties, and thereby raise them to new heights of being; we render them more liberal in the pursuit of wealth; we give them a zest for toil that mocks at danger, and enables them where honour the fair vision leads, to follow. (27) We fill their souls with deeper modesty, a self-constraint more staunch; about the things they care for most, there floats a halo of protecting awe. (28) Fools and unwise are they who choose not beauteous men to be their generals. How merrily would I, at any rate, march through fire by the side of Cleinias; (29) and so would all of you, I know full well, in company of him who now addresses you.

*(25) "We beauties."*

*(26) The {eispnelas} in relation to the {aitas}, the Inspirer to the Hearer. Cf. Theocr. xii. 13; Ael. "V. H." iii. 12. See Muller, "Dorians," ii. 300 foll.*

*(27) {philokaloterous}. Cf. Plat. "Phaedr." 248 D; "Criti." 111 E; Aristot. "Eth. N." iv. 4. 4; x. 9. 3.*

*(28) Lit. "they feel most awe of what they most desire."*

*(29) Cf. "Mem." I. iii. 9.*

Cease, therefore, your perplexity, O Socrates, abandon fears and doubts, believe and know that this thing of which I make great boast, my beauty, has power to confer some benefit on humankind.

Once more, let no man dare dishonour beauty, merely because the flower of it soon fades, since even as a child has growth in beauty, so is it with the stripling, the grown man, the reverend senior. (30) And this the proof of my contention. Whom do we choose to bear the sacred olive-shoot (31) in honour of Athena?—whom else save beautiful old men?

witnessing thereby (32) that beauty walks hand in hand as a companion with every age of life, from infancy to eld.

(30) Cf. ib. III. iii. 12.

(31) Cf. Aristoph. "Wasps," 544.

(32) Or, "beauty steps in attendance lovingly hand in hand at every season of the life of man." So Walt Whitman, passim.

Or again, if it be sweet to win from willing hearts the things we seek for, I am persuaded that, by the eloquence of silence, I could win a kiss from yonder girl or boy more speedily than ever you could, O sage! by help of half a hundred subtle arguments.

Eh, bless my ears, what's that? (Socrates broke in upon this final flourish of the speaker). So beautiful you claim to rival me, you boaster?

Crit. Why, yes indeed, I hope so, or else I should be uglier than all the Silenuses in the Satyric drama. (33)

(33) The MSS. add ("to whom, be it noted, Socrates indeed bore a marked resemblance"). Obviously a gloss. Cf. Aristoph. "Clouds," 224; Plat. "Symp." 215 B.

Good! (Socrates rejoined); the moment the programme of discussion is concluded, (34) please remember, we must obtain a verdict on the point of beauty. Judgment shall be given—not at the bar of Alexander, son of Priam—but of these (35) who, as you flatter yourself, have such a hankering to kiss you.

(34) Lit. "the arguments proposed have gone the round."

(35) i.e. "the boy and girl." Al. "the present company, who are so eager to bestow on you their kisses."

Oh, Socrates (he answered, deprecatingly), will you not leave it to the arbitrament of Cleinias?

Then Socrates: Will you never tire of repeating that one name? It is Cleinias here, there, and everywhere with you.

Crit. And if his name died on my lips, think you my mind would less recall his memory? Know you not, I bear so clear an image of him in my soul, that had I the sculptor's or the limner's skill, I might portray his features as exactly from this image of the mind as from contemplation of his actual self.

But Socrates broke in: Pray, why then, if you bear about this lively image, why do you give me so much trouble, dragging me to this and that place, where you hope to see him?

Crit. For this good reason, Socrates, the sight of him inspires gladness, whilst his phantom brings not joy so much as it engenders longing.

At this point Hermogenes protested: I find it most unlike you, Socrates, to treat thus negligently one so passion-crazed as Critobulus.

Socrates replied: Do you suppose the sad condition of the patient dates from the moment only of our intimacy?

Herm. Since when, then?

Soc. Since when? Why, look at him: the down begins to mantle on his cheeks, (36) and on the nape (37) of Cleinias' neck already mounts. The fact is, when they fared to the same school together, he caught the fever. This his father was aware of, and consigned him to me, hoping I might be able to do something for him. Ay, and his plight is not so sorry now. Once he would stand agape at him like one whose gaze is fixed upon the Gorgons, (38) his eyes one stony stare, and like a stone himself turn heavily away. But nowadays I have seen the statue actually blink. (39) And yet, may Heaven help me! my good sirs, I think, between ourselves, the culprit must have bestowed a kiss on Cleinias, than which love's flame asks no fiercer fuel. (40) So insatiable a thing it is and so suggestive of mad fantasy. (And for this reason held perhaps in higher honour, because of all external acts the close of lip with lip bears the same name as that of soul with soul in love.) (41) Wherefore, say I, let every one who wishes to be master of himself and sound of soul abstain from kisses imprinted on fair lips. (42)

(36) Lit. "*creeping down beside his ears.*" Cf. "*Od.*" xi. 319:

{prin sphoin upo krotaphoisin ioulous anthesai pukasai te genus euanthei lakhne.}

"*(Zeus destroyed the twain) ere the curls had bloomed beneath*

*their temples, and darked their chins with the blossom of youth.*"

—Butcher and Lang. Cf. Theocr. xv. 85: {praton ioulon apo

krotaphon kataballon}, "*with the first down upon his cheeks*"

(Lang); Aesch. "Theb." 534.

(37) {pros to opisthen}, perhaps = "ad posteriorem capitis partem," which would be more applicable to Critobulus, whose whiskers were just beginning to grow, than to Callias. Possibly we should read (after Pollux, ii. 10) {peri ten upenen}, "on the upper lip." See Plat. "Protag." 309 B; "Il." xxiv. 348; "Od." x. 279.

(38) Cf. Pind. "Pyth." x. 75.

(39) See "Cyrop." I. iv. 28; Shakesp. "Ven. and Ad." 89: "But when her lips were ready for his pay, he winks, and turns his lips another way."

(40) Or, "a kiss which is to passion as dry combustious matter is to fire," Shakesp. ib. 1162.

(41) Or, "is namesake of the love within the soul of lovers." The whole passage, involving a play on the words {philein phileisthai}, "where kisses rain without, love reigns within," is probably to be regarded as a gloss. Cf. "Mem." I. iii. 13.

(42) Cf. "Mem." I. iii. 8-14.

Then Charmides: Oh! Socrates, why will you scare your friends with these hobgoblin terrors, (43) bidding us all beware of handsome faces, whilst you yourself—yes, by Apollo, I will swear I saw you at the schoolmaster's (44) that time when both of you were poring over one book, in which you searched for something, you and Critobulus, head to head, shoulder to shoulder bare, as if incorporate? (45)

(43) Cf. Plat. "Crit." 46 D; "Hell." IV. iv. 17; Arist. "Birds," 1245.

*(44) "Grammarian's." Plat. "Protag." 312 B; 326 D; Dem. 315. 8.*

*(45) Like Hermia and Helena, "Mids. N. D." iii. 2. 208.*

As yes, alack the day! (he answered); and that is why, no doubt, my shoulder ached for more than five days afterwards, as if I had been bitten by some fell beast, and methought I felt a sort of scraping at the heart. (46) Now therefore, in the presence of these witnesses, I warn you, Critobulus, never again to touch me till you wear as thick a crop of hair (47) upon your chin as on your head.

*(46) Reading {knisma}, "scratching." Plat. "Hipp. maj." 304 A. Al.*

*{knesma}.*

*(47) See Jebb, "Theophr. Ch." xxiv. 16.*

So pell-mell they went at it, half jest half earnest, and so the medley ended. Callias here called on Charmides.

Call. Now, Charmides, it lies with you to tell us why you pride yourself on poverty. (48)

*(48) Zeune, cf. "Cyrop." VIII. iii. 35-50.*

Charmides responded: On all hands it is admitted, I believe, that confidence is better than alarm; better to be a freeman than a slave; better to be worshipped than pay court to others; better to be trusted than to be suspected by one's country.

Well now, I will tell you how it fared with me in this same city when I was wealthy. First, I lived in daily terror lest some burglar should break into my house and steal my goods and do myself some injury. I cringed before informers. (49) I was obliged to pay these people court, because I knew that I could injure them far less than they could injure me. Never-ending the claims upon my pocket which the state enforced upon me; and as to setting foot abroad, that was beyond the range of possibility. But now that I have lost my property across the frontier, (50) and derive no income from my lands in Attica itself; now that my very household goods have been sold up, I stretch my legs at ease, I get a good night's rest. The distrust of my fellow-citizens has vanished; instead of trembling at threats, it is now my turn to threaten; at last I feel myself a freeman, with liberty to go abroad or stay at home as suits my fancy. The tables now are turned. It is the rich who rise to give me their seats, who stand aside and make way for me as I meet them in the streets. To-day I am like a despot, yesterday I was literally a slave;

formerly it was I who had to pay my tribute (51) to the sovereign people, now it is I who am supported by the state by means of general taxation. (52)

*(49) "And police agents."*

*(50) Cf. "Mem." II. viii. 1.*

*(51) {phoros}, tributum. Al. "property-tax." Cf. "Econ." ii. 6.*

*(52) {telos}, vectigal. Sturz, "Lex. Xen." s.v. Cf. "Pol. Ath." i. 3.*

And there is another thing. So long as I was rich, they threw in my teeth as a reproach that I was friends with Socrates, but now that I am become a beggar no one troubles his head two straws about the matter. Once more, the while I rolled in plenty I had everything to lose, and, as a rule, I lost it; what the state did not exact, some mischance stole from me. But now that is over. I lose nothing, having nought to lose; but, on the contrary, I have everything to gain, and live in hope of some day getting something. (53)

*(53) "I feed on the pleasures of hope, and fortune in the future."*

Call. And so, of course, your one prayer is that you may never more be rich, and if you are visited by a dream of luck your one thought is to offer sacrifice to Heaven to avert misfortune. (54)

*(54) Or, "you wake up in a fright, and offer sacrifice to the*

*'Averters.'" For {tois apotropaiois} see Aristoph. "Plutus," 359;*

*Plat. "Laws," 854 B; "Hell." III. iii. 4.*

Char. No, that I do not. On the contrary, I run my head into each danger most adventurously. I endure, if haply I may see a chance of getting something from some quarter of the sky some day.

Come now (Socrates exclaimed), it lies with you, sir, you, Antisthenes, to explain to us, how it is that you, with means so scanty, make so loud a boast of wealth.

Because (he answered) I hold to the belief, sirs, that wealth and poverty do not lie in a man's estate, but in men's souls. Even in private life how many scores of people have I seen, who, although they roll in wealth, yet deem themselves so poor, there is nothing they will shrink from, neither toil nor danger, in order to add a little to their store. (55) I have known two brothers, (56) heirs to equal fortunes, one of whom has enough, more than enough, to cover his expenditure; the other is in absolute indigence. And so to monarchs, there are not a few, I perceive, so ravenous of wealth that they will outdo the veriest vagrants in atrocity. Want (57) prompts a thousand crimes, you must admit. Why do men steal? why break burglariously into houses? why hale men and women captive and make slaves of them? Is it not from want? Nay, there are monarchs who at one fell swoop destroy whole houses, make wholesale massacre, and oftentimes reduce entire states to slavery, and all for the sake of wealth. These I must needs pity for the cruel malady which plagues them. Their condition, to my mind, resembles that poor creature's who, in spite of all he has (58) and all he eats, can never stay the wolf that gnaws his vitals.

*(55) Cf. "Cyrop." VIII. ii. 21; Hor. "Epist." i. 2. 26, "semper avarus eget."*

*(56) Is Antisthenes thinking of Callias and Hermogenes? (presuming these are sons of Hipponicus and brothers). Cf. "Mem." II. x. 3.*

*(57) Or, "'Tis want that does it." See "Pol. Ath." i. 5; "Rev," i. 1.*

*(58) Reading {ekhon}, or if {pinon}, transl. "who eats and drinks, but never sates himself."*

But as to me, my riches are so plentiful I cannot lay my hands on them myself; (59) yet for all that I have enough to eat till my hunger is stayed, to drink till my thirst is sated; (60) to clothe myself withal; and out of doors not Callias there, with all his riches, is more safe than I from shivering; and when I find myself indoors, what warmer shirting (61) do I need than my bare walls? what ampler greatcoat than the tiles above my head? these seem to suit me well enough; and as to bedclothes, I am not so ill supplied but it is a business to arouse me in the morning.

*(59) "That I can scarce discover any portion of it." Zeune cf. "Econ." viii. 2.*

*(60) So "the master" himself. See "Mem." I. ii. 1, vi. 5.*

*(61) Cf. Aristot. "Pol." ii. 8. 1, of Hippodamus.*

And as to sexual desire, my body's need is satisfied by what comes first to hand. Indeed, there is no lack of warmth in the caress which greets me, just because it is unsought by others. (62)

*(62) Cf. "Mem." I. iii. 14, the germ of cynicism and stoicism, the*

*Socratic {XS} form of "better to marry than to burn."*

Well then, these several pleasures I enjoy so fully that I am much more apt to pray for less than more of them, so strongly do I feel that some of them are sweeter than what is good for one or profitable.

But of all the precious things in my possession, I reckon this the choicest, that were I robbed of my whole present stock, there is no work so mean, but it would amply serve me to furnish me with sustenance. Why, look you, whenever I desire to fare delicately, I have not to purchase precious viands in the market, which becomes expensive, but I open the storehouse of my soul, and dole them out. (63) Indeed, as far as pleasure goes, I find it better to await desire before I suffer meat or drink to pass my lips, than to have recourse to any of your costly viands, as, for instance, now, when I have chanced on this fine Thasian wine, (64) and sip it without thirst. But indeed, the man who makes frugality, not wealth of worldly goods, his aim, is on the face of it a much more upright person. And why?—the man who is content with what he has will least of all be prone to clutch at what is his neighbour's.

*(63) Or, "turn to the storehouse of a healthy appetite." See "Apol."*

*18, the same sentiment "ex ore Socratis."*

*(64) See Athen. "Deipnos." i. 28.*

And here's a point worth noting. Wealth of my sort will make you liberal of soul. Look at Socrates; from him it was I got these riches. He did not supply me with it by weight or by measure, but just as much as I could carry, he with bounteous hand consigned to me. And I, too, grudge it to no man now. To all my friends without distinction I am ready to display my opulence: come one, come all; and whosoever likes to take a share is welcome to the wealth that lies within my soul. Yes, and moreover, that most luxurious of possessions, (65) unbroken leisure, you can see, is mine, which leaves me free to contemplate things worthy of contemplation, (66) and to drink in with my ears all charming sounds. And what I value most, freedom to spend whole days in pure scholastic intercourse (67) with Socrates, to whom I am devoted. (68) And he, on his side, is not the person to admire those whose tale of gold and silver happens to be the largest, but those who are well-pleasing to him he chooses for companions, and will consort with to the end.

*(65) See Eur. "Ion," 601. Lit. "at every moment I command it."*

*(66) "To gaze upon all fairest shows (like a spectator in the theatre), and to drink in sounds most delectable." So Walt Whitman.*

*(67) Aristot. "Rhet." ii. 4. 12; "Eth. N." ix. 4. 9.*

*(68) See "Mem." III. xi. 17.*

With these words the speaker ended, and Callias exclaimed:

By Hera, I envy you your wealth, Antisthenes, firstly, because the state does not lay burthens on you and treat you like a slave; and secondly, people do not fall into a rage with you when you refuse to be their creditor.

You may stay your envy (interposed Niceratus), I shall presently present myself to borrow of him this same key of his to independence. (69) Trained as I am to cast up figures by my master Homer—

*Seven tripods, which ne'er felt the fire, and of gold ten talents*

*And burnished braziers twenty, and horses twelve—* (70)

by weight and measure duly reckoned, (71) I cannot stay my craving for enormous wealth. And that's the reason certain people, I daresay, imagine I am inordinately fond of riches.

*(69) Or, "his want-for-nothing," or, "supply-all."*

*(70) Niceratus quotes "Il." ix. 122, 123, 263, 264.*

*(71) Or, "by number and by measure," "so much apiece, so much a pound," in reference to Antisthenes' remark that Socrates does not stint his "good things."*

The remark drew forth a peal of laughter from the company, who thought the speaker hit the truth exactly.

Then some one: It lies with you, Hermogenes, to tell us who your friends are; and next, to demonstrate the greatness of their power and their care for you, if you would prove to us your right to pride yourself on them.

Herm. That the gods know all things, that the present and the future lie before their eyes, are tenets held by Hellenes and barbarians alike. This is obvious; or else, why do states and nations, one and all, inquire of the gods by divination what they ought to do and what they ought not? This also is apparent, that we believe them able to do us good and to do us harm; or why do all men pray to Heaven to avert the evil and bestow the good? Well then, my boast is that these gods, who know and can do all things, (72) deign to be my friends; so that, by reason of their care for me, I can never escape from their sight, (73) neither by night nor by day, whithersoever I essay to go, whatsoever I take in hand to do. (74) But because they know beforehand the end and issue of each event, they give me signals, sending messengers, be it some voice, (75) or vision of the night, with omens of the solitary bird, which tell me what I should and what I should not do. When I listen to their warnings all goes well with me, I have no reason to repent; but if, as ere now has been the case, I have been disobedient, chastisement has overtaken me.

*(72) Cf. "Mem." I. i. 19; I. iv. 18.*

*(73) Schneid. cf. Hom. "Il." x. 279, {oude se letho kinomenos}, "nor doth any motion of mine escape thee" (A. Lang); and see Arrian, "Epictet." i. 12. 3.*

*(74) Cf. Ps. cxxxix. "Domine probasti."*

*(75) See "Mem." I. i. 3; "Apol." xii. 13; "Cyrop." VIII. vii. 3.*

Then Socrates: All this I well believe, (76) but there is one thing I would gladly learn of you: What service do you pay the gods, so to secure their friendship?

*(76) Lit. "Nay, nought of the things you tell us is incredible, but..."*

Truly it is not a ruinous service, Socrates (he answered)—far from it. I give them thanks, which is not costly. I make return to them of all they give to me from time to time. I speak well of them, with all the strength I have. And whenever I take their sacred names to witness, I do not wittingly falsify my word.

Then God be praised (said Socrates), if being what you are, you have such friends; the gods themselves, it would appear, delight in nobleness of soul. (77)

(77) {kalokagathia}, "beautiful and gentle manhood."

Thus, in solemn sort, the theme was handled, thus gravely ended.

But now it was the jester's turn, and so they fell to asking him: (78) What could he see to pride himself upon so vastly in the art of making people laugh?

(78) Lit. "now that they had come to Philippus (in the 'period' of

discussion), they..." Or read, after Hartman, "An. Xen." p.

242, {eken} (sc. {o logos}).

Surely I have good reason (he replied). The whole world knows my business is to set them laughing, so when they are in luck's way, they eagerly invite me to a share of it; but if ill betide them, helter-skelter off they go, and never once turn back, (79) so fearful are they I may set them laughing will he nill he.

(79) Plat. "Rep." 620 E; "Laws," 854 C.

Nic. Heavens! you have good reason to be proud; with me it is just the opposite. When any of my friends are doing well, they take good care to turn their backs on me, (80) but if ever it goes ill with them, they claim relationship by birth, (81) and will not let their long-lost cousin out of sight.

(80) Or, "they take good care to get out of my way," "they hold aloof

from me entirely."

(81) Or, "produce the family-pedigree and claim me for a cousin." Cf.

Lucian v., "Tim." 49; Ter. "Phorm." ii. 33, 45.

Charm. Well, well! and you, sir (turning to the Syracusan), what do you pride yourself upon? No doubt, upon the boy?

The Syr. Not I, indeed; I am terribly afraid concerning him. It is plain enough to me that certain people are contriving for his ruin. (82)

(82) {diaphtheirai} = (1) to destroy, make away with; (2) to ruin and corrupt, seduce by bribes or otherwise.

Good gracious! (83) (Socrates exclaimed, when he heard that), what crime can they conceive your boy is guilty of that they should wish to make an end of him?

(83) Lit. "Heracles!" "Zounds!"

The Syr. I do not say they want to murder him, but wheedle him away with bribes to pass his nights with them.

Soc. And if that happened, you on your side, it appears, believe the boy will be corrupted?

The Syr. Beyond all shadow of a doubt, most villainously.

Soc. And you, of course, you never dream of such a thing. You don't spend nights with him?

The Syr. Of course I do, all night and every night.

Soc. By Hera, what a mighty piece of luck (84) for you—to be so happily compounded, of such flesh and blood. You alone can't injure those who sleep beside you. You have every right, it seems, to boast of your own flesh, if nothing else.

(84) Cf. Plat. "Symp." 217 A.

The Syr. Nay, in sooth, it is not on that I pride myself.

Soc. Well, on what then?

The Syr. Why, on the silly fools who come and see my puppet show. (85) I live on them.

(85) "My marionettes." Cf. Herod. ii. 48; Lucian lxxii., "De Syr. d."

16; Aristot. "de Mund." 6.

Phil. Ah yes! and that explains how the other day I heard you praying to the gods to grant you, wheresoe'er you chance to be, great store of corn and wine, but dearth of wits. (86)

(86) Or, "of fruits abundance, but of wits a famine." Cf. Plat. "Rep."

546 A. His prayer resembles that of the thievish trader in Ovid,

"Fast." v. 675 foll., "Grant me to-day my daily... fraud!" but

in spite of himself (like Dogberry), he seems to pray to the gods

to "write him down an ass"!

Pass on (said Callias); now it is your turn, Socrates. What have you to say to justify your choice? How can you boast of so discredited an art? (87)

*(87) Sc. "the hold-door trade."*

He answered: Let us first decide (88) what are the duties of the good go-between; (89) and please to answer every question without hesitating; let us know the points to which we mutually assent. (90) Are you agreed to that?

*(88) Or, "define in common." Cf. "Mem." IV. vi. 15.*

*(89) Or, "man-praiser." Cf. "The Manx Witch," p. 47 (T. E. Brown),*

*"And Harry, more like a dooiney-molla For Jack, lak helpin him to*

*woo." See, too, Mr. Hall Caine's "Manxman," p. 73.*

*(90) See Plat. "Rep." 342 D, for a specimen of Socratic procedure,*

*"from one point of agreement to another."*

The Company, in chorus. Without a doubt (they answered, and the formula, once started, was every time repeated by the company, full chorus).

Soc. Are you agreed it is the business of a good go-between to make him (or her) on whom he plies his art agreeable to those with them? (91)

*(91) Al. "their followers." See "Mem." II. vi. 36.*

Omnes. Without a doubt.

Soc. And, further, that towards agreeableness, one step at any rate consists in wearing a becoming fashion of the hair and dress? (92) Are you agreed to that?

*(92) See Becker, "Char." Exc. iii. to Sc. xi.*

Omnes. Without a doubt.

Soc. And we know for certain, that with the same eyes a man may dart a look of love or else of hate (93) on those he sees. Are you agreed?

*(93) See "Mem." III. x. 5.*

Omnes. Without a doubt.

Soc. Well! and with the same tongue and lips and voice may speak with modesty or boastfulnes?

Omnes. Without a doubt.

Soc. And there are words that bear the stamp of hate, and words that tend to friendliness? (94)

(94) Cf. Ep. St. James iii. 10, "Out of the same mouth proceedeth

blessing and cursing."

Omnes. Without a doubt.

Soc. The good go-between will therefore make his choice between them, and teach only what conduces to agreeableness?

Omnes. Without a doubt.

Soc. And is he the better go-between who can make his clients pleasing to one person only, or can make them pleasing to a number? (95)

(95) Or, "to the many." The question is ambiguous. $\{e\}$ = "an" or

"quam."

The company was here divided; the one half answered, "Yes, of course, the largest number," whilst the others still maintained, "Without a doubt."

And Socrates, remarking, "That proposition is agreed to also," thus proceeded: And if further he were able to make them pleasing to the whole community, should we not have found in this accomplished person an arch-go-between?

Clearly so (they answered with one voice).

Soc. If then a man had power to make his clients altogether pleasing; that man, I say, might justly pride himself upon his art, and should by rights receive a large reward? (96)

(96) Or, "he deserves to do a rattling business," "to take handsome

fees." Cf. Sheridan's Mrs. Coupler, in "A Trip to Scarborough."

And when these propositions were agreed to also, he turned about and said: Just such a man, I take it, is before you in the person of Antisthenes! (97)

(97) See Diog. Laert. "Antisth." VI. i. 8; Plut. "Symp." ii. 1. 503.

Whereupon Antisthenes exclaimed: What! are you going to pass on the business? will you devolve this art of yours on me as your successor, Socrates? (98)

(98) Or, "going to give up business, and hand on the trade to me as

*your successor?"*

I will, upon my word, I will (he answered): since I see that you have practised to some purpose, nay elaborated, an art which is the handmaid to this other.

And what may that be? asked Antisthenes.

Soc. The art of the procurer. (99)

*(99) Cf. Plat. "Theaet." 150 A; Aristot. "Eth. N." v. 2, 13; Aeschin.*

*3, 7; Plut. "Solon," 23.*

The other (in a tone of deep vexation): Pray, what thing of the sort are you aware I ever perpetrated?

Soc. I am aware that it was you who introduced our host here, Callias, to that wise man Prodicus; (100) they were a match, you saw, the one enamoured of philosophy, and the other in need of money. It was you again, I am well enough aware, who introduced him once again to Hippias (101) of Elis, from whom he learnt his "art of memory"; (102) since which time he has become a very ardent lover, (103) from inability to forget each lovely thing he sets his eyes on. And quite lately, if I am not mistaken, it was you who sounded in my ears such praise of our visitor from Heraclea, (104) that first you made me thirst for his society, and then united us. (105) For which indeed I am your debtor, since I find him a fine handsome fellow and true gentleman. (106) And did you not, moreover, sing the praises of Aeschylus of Phlius (107) in my ears and mine in his?—in fact, affected us so much by what you said, we fell in love and took to coursing wildly in pursuit of one another like two dogs upon a trail. (108)

*(100) Or, "the sage," "the sophist." See "Mem." I. vi. 13; II. i. 21.*

*(101) See "Mem." IV. iv. 5; and for his art of memory cf. Plat. "Hipp.*
   *min." 368 D; "Hipp. maj." 285 E.*

*(102) The "memoria technica" (see Aristot. "de An." iii. 3, 6), said*
   *to have been invented by Simonides of Ceos. Cic. "de Or." ii. 86;*
   *"de Fin." ii. 32; Quinct. xi. 2. 559.*

*(103) Or, "has grown amorous to a degree" (al. "an adept in love's*

lore himself." Cf. Plat. "Rep." 474 D, "an authority in love."—
Jowett) "for the simple reason he can't forget each lovely thing
he once has seen." Through the "ars memoriae" of Hippias, it
becomes an "idee fixe" of the mind.

(104) Perhaps Zeuxippus. See Plat. "Prot." 318 B. Al. Zeuxis, also a
native of Heraclea. See "Mem." I. iv. 3; "Econ." x. 1.

(105) Or, "introduced him to me." Cf. "Econ." iii. 14; Plat. "Lach."
200 D.

(106) "An out-and-out {kalos te kagathos}."

(107) Who this Phliasian is, no one knows.

(108) Al. "like two hounds chevying after one another."

With such examples of your wonder-working skill before my eyes, I must suppose you are a first-rate matchmaker. For consider, a man with insight to discern two natures made to be of service to each other, and with power to make these same two people mutually enamoured! That is the sort of man, I take it, who should weld together states in friendship; cement alliances with gain to the contracting parties; (109) and, in general, be found an acquisition to those several states; to friends and intimates, and partisans in war, a treasure worth possessing. (110) But you, my friend, you got quite angry. One would suppose I had given you an evil name in calling you a first-rate matchmaker.

(109) Al. "and cement desirable matrimonial connections." Cf. Aristot.
"Pol." iii. 9, 13. 1280 B; v. 4, 5-8. 1303 B.

(110) See the conversation with Critobulus, so often referred to,
{peri philias}, in "Mem." II. vi.

Yes (he answered meekly), but now I am calm. It is clear enough, if I possess these powers I shall find myself surcharged with spiritual riches.

In this fashion the cycle of the speeches was completed. (111)

*(111) See Hug, "Einleitung," xxxi. "Quellen des Platonischen*

*Symposion."*

V

Then Callias: Our eyes are on you, Critobulus. Yours to enter the lists (1) against the champion Socrates, who claims the prize of beauty. Do you hesitate?

*(1) Soph. "Fr." 234; Thuc. i. 93.*

Soc. Likely enough he does, for possibly he sees Sir Pandarus stands high in their esteem who are the judges of the contest.

In spite of which (retorted Critobulus), I am not for drawing back. (2) I am ready; so come on, and if you have any subtle argument to prove that you are handsomer than I am, now's your time, instruct us. But just stop one minute; have the goodness, please, to bring the lamp a little closer.

*(2) Or, "I do; but all the same, I am not for shirking." Cf. Aristoph.*

*"Frogs," 860, {etiomos eum egoge, kouk anaduomai, daknein}: "I'm*

*up to it; I am resolved" (Frere); Dem. "de F. Leg." 406 20: "His*

*resolution never reached that point, but shrank back, for his*

*conscience checked it" (Kennedy).*

Soc. Well then, I call upon you first of all, as party to this suit, to undergo the preliminary examination. (3) Attend to what I say, and please be good enough to answer.

*(3) The {anakrisis}, or "previous inquiry" (before one of the archons)*

*of parties concerned in a suit, to see whether the action lay. Cf.*

*Plat. "Charm." 176 C. See Gow, "Companion," xiv. 74.*

Crit. Do you be good enough yourself to put your questions.

Soc. Do you consider that the quality of beauty is confined to man, or is it to be found in other objects also? What is your belief on this point?

Crit. For my part, I consider it belongs alike to animals—the horse, the ox—and to many things inanimate: that is to say, a shield, a sword, a spear are often beautiful.

Soc. How is it possible that things, in no respect resembling one another, should each and all be beautiful? (4)

*(4) See "Mem." III. viii. 5, quoted by Galen, "de Usu Part." i. 370.*

Crit. Of course it is, God bless me! if well constructed by the hand of man to suit the sort of work for which we got them, or if naturally adapted to satisfy some want, the things in either case are beautiful.

Soc. Can you tell me, then, what need is satisfied by our eyes?

Crit. Clearly, the need of vision.

Soc. If so, my eyes are proved at once to be more beautiful than yours.

Crit. How so?

Soc. Because yours can only see just straight in front of them, whereas mine are prominent and so projecting, they can see aslant. (5)

*(5) Or, "squint sideways and command the flanks."*

Crit. And amongst all animals, you will tell us that the crab has loveliest eyes? (6) Is that your statement?

*(6) Or, "is best provided in respect of eyeballs."*

Soc. Decidedly, the creature has. And all the more so, since for strength and toughness its eyes by nature are the best constructed.

Crit. Well, let that pass. To come to our two noses, which is the more handsome, yours or mine?

Soc. Mine, I imagine, if, that is, the gods presented us with noses for the sake of smelling. Your nostrils point to earth; but mine are spread out wide and flat, as if to welcome scents from every quarter.

Crit. But consider, a snubness of the nose, how is that more beautiful than straightness? (7)

*(7) Or, "your straight nose." Cf. Plat. "Theaet." 209 C: Soc. "Or, if I had further known you not only as having nose and eyes, but as having a snub nose and prominent eyes, should I have any more notion of you than myself and others who resemble me?" Cf. also Aristot. "Pol." v. 9, 7: "A nose which varies from the ideal of straightness to a hook or snub may still be a good shape and agreeable to the eye; but if the excess be very great, all*

*symmetry is lost, and the nose at last ceases to be a nose at all on account of some excess in one direction or defect in the other; and this is true of every other part of the human body. The same law of proportion holds in states."—Jowett.*

Soc. For this good reason, that a snub nose does not discharge the office of a barrier; (8) it allows the orbs of sight free range of vision: whilst your towering nose looks like an insulting wall of partition to shut off the two eyes. (9)

*(8) Or, "the humble snub is not a screen or barricade."*

*(9) Cf. "Love's Labour Lost," v. 2. 568: Boyet. "Your nose says no, you are not, for it stands too right"; also "The Song of Solomon," vii. 4: "Thy nose is the tower of Lebanon, which looketh toward Damascus."*

As to the mouth (proceeded Critobulus), I give in at once; for, given mouths are made for purposes of biting, you could doubtless bite off a much larger mouthful with your mouth than I with mine.

Soc. Yes, and you will admit, perhaps, that I can give a softer kiss than you can, thanks to my thick lips.

Crit. It seems I have an uglier mouth than any ass.

Soc. And here is a fact which you will have to reckon with, if further evidence be needed to prove that I am handsomer than you. The naiads, nymphs, divine, have as their progeny Sileni, who are much more like myself, I take it, than like you. Is that conclusive?

Nay, I give it up (cried Critobulus), I have not a word to say in answer. I am silenced. Let them record the votes. I fain would know at once what I must suffer or must pay. (10) Only (he added) let them vote in secret. (11) I am afraid your wealth and his (Antisthenes') combined may overpower me.

*(10) For this formula see "Dict. Ant." {timema}. Cf. "Econ." xi. 25; Plat. "Apol." 36 B; "Statesm." 299 A; "Laws," freq.; Dem. 529. 23; 533. 2.*

*(11) And not as in the case described (Thuc. iv. 74), where the people*

*(at Megara) were compelled to give sentence on the political*

*opponents of the oligarchs by an open vote. Cf. Lysias, 133, 12,*

*{ten de psephon ouk eis kadiskous, alla phaneran epi tas trapezas*

*tautas dei tithenai}.*

Accordingly the boy and girl began to register the votes in secret, while Socrates directed the proceedings. He would have the lamp-stand (12) this time brought close up to Critobulus; the judges must on no account be taken in; the victor in the suit would get from the two judges, not a wreath of ribands (13) for a chaplet, but some kisses.

*(12) {ton lukhnon} here, above, S. 2, {ton lamptera}. Both, I take it,*

*are oil-lamps, and differ merely as "light" and "lamp."*

*(13) Cf. Plat. "Symp." 213; "Hell." V. i. 3.*

When the urns were emptied, it was found that every vote, without exception, had been cast for Critobulus. (14)

*(14) Lit. "When the pebbles were turned out and proved to be with*

*Critobulus, Socrates remarked, 'Papae!'" which is as much to say,*

*"Od's pity!"*

Whereat Socrates: Bless me! you don't say so? The coin you deal in, Critobulus, is not at all like that of Callias. His makes people just; whilst yours, like other filthy lucre, can corrupt both judge and jury. (15)

*(15) {kai dikastas kai kritas}, "both jury and presiding judges," i.e.*

*the company and the boy and girl.*

## VI

Thereupon some members of the party called on Critobulus to accept the meed of victory in kisses (due from boy and girl); others urged him first to bribe their master; whilst others bandied other jests. Amidst the general hilarity Hermogenes alone kept silence.

Whereat Socrates turned to the silent man, and thus accosted him: Hermogenes, what is a drunken brawl? Can you explain to us?

He answered: If you ask me what it is, I do not know, but I can tell you what it seems to me to be.

Soc. That seems as good. What does it seem?

Her. A drunken brawl, in my poor judgment, is annoyance caused to people over wine.

Soc. Are you aware that you at present are annoying us by silence?

Her. What, whilst you are talking?

Soc. No, when we pause a while.

Her. Then you have not observed that, as to any interval between your talk, a man would find it hard to insert a hair, much more one grain of sense.

Then Socrates: O Callias, to the rescue! help a man severely handled by his cross-examiner.

Call. With all my heart (and as he spoke he faced Hermogenes). Why, when the flute is talking, we are as silent as the grave.

Her. What, would you have me imitate Nicostratus (1) the actor, reciting his tetrameters (2) to the music of the fife? Must I discourse to you in answer to the flute?

*(1) See Cobet, "Pros. Xen." p. 53; and cf. Diog. Laert. iv. 3, 4;*

*Polyaen. vi. 10; "Hell." IV. viii. 18.*

*(2) See Aristoph. "Clouds," where Socrates is giving Strepsiades a*

*lesson in "measures," 639-646: {poteron to trimetron e to*

*tetrametron}.*

Then Socrates: By all that's holy, I wish you would, Hermogenes. How delightful it would be. Just as a song sounds sweeter in concert with the flute, so would your talk be more mellifluous attuned to its soft pipings; and particularly if you would use gesticulation like the flute-girl, to suit the tenor of your speech.

Here Callias demanded: And when our friend (Antisthenes) essays to cross-examine people (3) at a banquet, what kind of piping (4) should he have?

*(3) Or, "a poor body," in reference to the elentic onslaught made on*

*himself by Antisthenes above.*

*(4) {to aulema}, a composition for reed instruments, "music for the*

flute." Cf. Aristoph. "Frogs," 1302.

Ant. The person in the witness-box would best be suited with a serpent-hissing theme. (5)

(5) Or, "motif on a scrannel pipe." See L. & S. s.v. {puthaules}. Cf.

Poll. iv. 81, {puthikon aulema}, an air ({nomos}) played on the

{puthois aulos}, expressing the battle between Apollo and the

Python, the hiss of which was imitated.

Thus the stream of talk flowed on; until the Syracusan, who was painfully aware that while the company amused themselves, his "exhibition" was neglected, turned, in a fit of jealous spleen, at last on Socrates. (6)

(6) "The Syracusan is 'civil as an orange, and of that jealous

complexion.'"

The Syr. They call you Socrates. Are you that person commonly nicknamed the thinker? (7)

(7) Apparently he has been to see the "Clouds" (exhibited first in 423

B.C.), and has conceived certain ideas concerning Socrates, "a

wise man, who speculated about the heaven above, and searched into

the earth beneath, and made the worse appear the better cause."

Plat. "Apol." 18 B, 19 C. "Clouds," 101, 360, {khair o presbuta

... ton nun meteorosophiston... ta te meteora phrontistes}.

Soc. Which surely is a better fate than to be called a thoughtless person?

The Syr. Perhaps, if you were not thought to split your brains on things above us—transcendental stuff. (8)

(8) Or, "if only you were held to be less 'meteoric,' less head-in-

airy in your speculations."

Soc. And is there anything more transcendental than the gods?

The Syr. By heaven! no, it is not the gods above us whom you care for, but for matters void of use and valueless. (9)

(9) It is impossible to give the play on words. The Syr.

{anophelestaton}. Soc. {ano... ophelousin}. Schenkl after

Madvig emend.: {ton ano en nephelais onton} = "but for things in *the clouds above."*

Soc. It seems, then, by your showing I do care for them. How value less the gods, not more, if being above us they make the void of use to send us rain, and cause their light to shine on us? And now, sir, if you do not like this frigid (10) argument, why do you cause me trouble? The fault is yours. (11)

*(10) Cf. "Cyrop." VIII. iv. 22, 23.*

*(11) {pho parekhousin... pragmata moi parekhon}. Lit. "cause light*

*... causing me trouble."*

Well, let that be (the other answered); answer me one question: How many fleas' feet distance is it, pray, from you to me? (12) They say you measure them by geometric scale.

*(12) See Aristoph. "Clouds," 144 foll.:*

{aneret' arti Khairephonta Sokrates psullan oposous alloito tous autes podas dakousa gar...}

*Cf. Lucian, ii. "Prom. in Verb. 6," and "Hudibras, the Second Part*

*of," canto iii.:*

How many scores a Flea will jump Of his own length from Head to Rump Which Socrates and Chaerephon In vain essayed so long agon.

But here Antisthenes, appealing to Philippus, interposed: You are a man full of comparisons. (13) Does not this worthy person strike you as somewhat like a bully seeking to pick a quarrel? (14)

*(13) Like Biron, "L. L. L." v. 2. 854. Or, "you are a clever*

*caricaturist." See Plat. "Symp." 215 A; Hug, "Enleitung," xiv.;*

*Aristoph. "Birds," 804 (Frere, p. 173); "Wasps," 1309.*

*(14) Aristoph. "Frogs," 857, "For it ill beseems illustrious bards to*

*scold like market-women." (Frere, p. 269); "Knights," 1410, "to*

*bully"; "Eccles." 142:*

{kai loidorountai g' osper empepokotes, kai ton paroinount' ekpherous' oi toxotai.}

Yes (replied the jester), he has a striking likeness to that person and a heap of others. He bristles with metaphors.

Soc. For all that, do not you be too eager to draw comparisons at his expense, or you will find yourself the image of a scold and brawler. (15)

*(15) Or, "a striking person."*

Phil. But what if I compare him to all the primest creatures of the world, to beauty's nonpareils, (16) to nature's best—I might be justly likened to a flatterer but not a brawler. (17)

*(16) Lit. "compare him to those in all things beauteous and the best."*

*With {tois pasi kalois kai tois beltistois} cf. Thuc. v. 28, {oi*

*'Argeioi arista eskhon tois pasi}, "The Argives were in excellent*

*condition in all respects." As to Philippus's back-handed*

*compliment to the showman, it reminds one of Peter Quince's*

*commendation of Bottom: "Yea and the best person too; and he is a*

*very paramour for a sweet voice."*

*(17) It is not easy to keep pace with the merryman's jests; but if I*

*follow his humour, he says to Socrates: "If the cap is to fit, you*

*must liken me to one who quits 'assault and battery' for*

*'compliments (sotto voce, "lies") and flattery.'"*

Soc. Why now, you are like a person apt to pick a quarrel, since you imply they are all his betters. (18)

*(18) When Socrates says {ei pant' autou beltio phes einai, k.t.l.},*

*the sense seems to be: "No, if you say that all these prime*

*creatures are better than he is, you are an abusive person still."*

Phil. What, would you have me then compare him to worse villains?

Soc. No, not even to worse villains.

Phil. What, then, to nothing, and to nobody?

Soc. To nought in aught. Let him remain his simple self—

Phil. Incomparable. But if my tongue is not to wag, whatever shall I do to earn my dinner?

Soc. Why, that you shall quite easily, if with your wagging tongue you do not try to utter things unutterable.

Here was a pretty quarrel over wine soon kindled and soon burnt.

VII

But on the instant those who had not assisted in the fray gave tongue, the one part urging the jester to proceed with his comparisons, and the other part dissuading.

The voice of Socrates was heard above the tumult: Since we are all so eager to be heard at once, what fitter time than now to sing a song, in chorus.

And suiting the action to the words, he commenced a stave.

The song was barely finished, when a potter's wheel was brought in, on which the dancing-girl was to perform more wonders.

At this point Socrates addressed the man of Syracuse: It seems I am likely to deserve the title which you gave me of a thinker in good earnest. Just now I am speculating by what means your boy and girl may pass a happy time, and we spectators still derive the greatest pleasure from beholding them; and this, I take it, is precisely what you would yourself most wish. Now I maintain, that throwing somersaults in and out of swords is a display of danger uncongenial to a banquet. And as for writing and reading on a wheel that all the while keeps whirling, I do not deny the wonder of it, but what pleasure such a marvel can present, I cannot for the life of me discover. Nor do I see how it is a whit more charming to watch these fair young people twisting about their bodies and imitating wheels than to behold them peacefully reposing.

We need not fare far afield to light on marvels, if that is our object. All about us here is full of marvel; we can begin at once by wondering, why it is the candle gives a light by dint of its bright flame, while side by side with it the bright bronze vessel gives no light, but shows within itself those other objects mirrored. (1) Or, how is it that oil, being moist and liquid, keeps that flame ablaze, but water, just because it is liquid, quenches fire. But no more do these same marvels tend to promote the object of the wine-cup. (2)

*(1) Cf. "Mem." IV. vii. 7. Socrates' criticism of Anaxagoras' theory*

 *with regard to the sun.*


*(2) Lit. "work to the same end as wine."*

But now, supposing your young people yonder were to tread a measure to the flute, some pantomime in dance, like those which the Graces and the Hours with the Nymphs are made to tread in pictures, (3) I think they would spend a far more happy time themselves, and our banquet would at once assume a grace and charm unlooked for.

*(3) Cf. Plat. "Laws," vii. 815 C; Hor. "Carm." i. 4. 6:*

iunctaeque Nymphis Gratiae decentes alterno terram quatiunt pede.

The Graces and the Nymphs, together knit, With rhythmic feet the meadow beat (Conington).

*Ib. iv. 7. 5.*

The Syracusan caught the notion readily.

By all that's holy, Socrates (he cried), a capital suggestion, and for my part, I warrant you, I will put a piece upon the stage, which will delight you, one and all.

## VIII

With these words the Syracusan made his exit, bent on organising his performance. (1) As soon as he was gone, Socrates once more essayed a novel argument. (2) He thus addressed them:

*(1) {sunekroteito}, "on the composition of his piece." Al. "amidst a*

*round of plaudits."*

*(2) "Struck the keynote of a novel theme." Cf. Plat. "Symp." 177 E.*

It were but reasonable, sirs, on our part not to ignore the mighty power here present, (3) a divinity in point of age coequal with the everlasting gods, yet in outward form the youngest, (4) who in magnitude embraces all things, and yet his shrine is planted in the soul of man. Love (5) is his name! and least of all should we forget him who are one and all votaries of this god. (6) For myself I cannot name the time at which I have not been in love with some one. (7) And Charmides here has, to my knowledge, captivated many a lover, while his own soul has gone out in longing for the love of not a few himself. (8) So it is with Critobulus also; the beloved of yesterday is become the lover of to-day. Ay, and Niceratus, as I am told, adores his wife, and is by her adored. (9) As to Hermogenes, which of us needs to be told (10) that the soul of this fond lover is consumed with passion for a fair ideal—call it by what name you will—the spirit blent of nobleness and beauty. (11) See you not what chaste severity dwells on his brow; (12) how tranquil his gaze; (13) how moderate his words; how gentle his intonation;

now radiant his whole character. And if he enjoys the friendship of the most holy gods, he keeps a place in his regard for us poor mortals. But how is it that you alone, Antisthenes, you misanthrope, love nobody?

(3) Cf. Shelley, "Hymn to Intellectual Beauty":

The awful shadow of some unseen Power Floats, though unseen, among us....

(4) Reading with L. D. after Blomfield (Aesch. "Ag." p. 304), {idrumenou}, or if as vulg. {isoumenou}, transl. "but in soul is fashioned like to mortal man."

(5) "Eros."

(6) Or, "who are each and all of us members of his band." For {thiasotai} cf. Aristot. "Eth. N." viii. 9. 5; Aristoph. "Frogs," 327.

(7) Cf. Plat. "Symp." 177 D: "No one will vote against you, Erysimachus, said Socrates; on the only subject ({ta erotika}) of which I profess to have any knowledge, I certainly cannot refuse to speak, nor, I presume, Agathon and Pasuanias; and there can be no doubt of Arisophanes, who is the constant servant of Dionysus and Aphrodite; nor will any one disagree of those I see around me" (Jowett).

(8) Or, "has had many a passionate admirer, and been enamoured of more than one true love himself." See Plat. "Charm.," ad in.

(9) For Love and Love-for-Love, {eros} and {anteros}, see Plat. "Phaedr." 255 D. Cf. Aristot. "Eth. N." ix. 1.

*(10) Lit. "which of us but knows his soul is melting away with passion." Cf. Theocr. xiv. 26.*

*(11) Lit. "beautiful and gentle manhood."*

*(12) Lit. "how serious are his brows."*

*(13) The phrases somehow remind one of Sappho's famous ode:*
{phainetai moi kenos isos theoisin emmen oner, ostis enantios toi izanei, kai plasion adu phoneusas upakouei kai gelasas imeroen}.

*But there we must stop. Hermogenes is a sort of Sir Percivale,*

"such a courtesy spake thro' the limbs and in the voice."

Nay, so help me Heaven! (he replied), but I do love most desperately yourself, O Socrates!

Whereat Socrates, still carrying on the jest, with a coy, coquettish air, (14) replied: Yes; only please do not bother me at present. I have other things to do, you see.

*(14) Al. "like a true coquet." Cf. Plat. "Phaedr." 228 C.*

Antisthenes replied: How absolutely true to your own character, arch go-between! (15) It is always either your familiar oracle won't suffer you, that's your pretext, and so you can't converse with me; or you are bent upon something or somebody else.

*(15) See "Mem." III. xi. 14.*

Then Socrates: For Heaven's sake, don't carbonado (16) me, Antisthenes, that's all. Any other savagery on your part I can stand, and will stand, as a lover should. However (he added), the less we say about your love the better, since it is clearly an attachment not to my soul, but to my lovely person.

*(16) Or, "tear and scratch me."*

And then, turning to Callias: And that you, Callias, do love Autolycus, this whole city knows and half the world besides, (17) if I am not mistaken; and the reason is that you are both sons of famous fathers, and yourselves illustrious. For my part I have ever admired your nature, but now much more so, when I see that you are in love with one who does not wanton in

- 53 -

luxury or languish in effeminacy, (18) but who displays to all his strength, his hardihood, his courage, and sobriety of soul. To be enamoured of such qualities as these is a proof itself of a true lover's nature.

*(17) Lit. "many a foreign visitor likewise."*

*(18) See the Attic type of character, as drawn by Pericles, Thuc. ii. 40.*

Whether indeed Aphrodite be one or twain (19) in personality, the heavenly and the earthly, I cannot tell, for Zeus, who is one and indivisible, bears many titles. (20) But this thing I know, that these twain have separate altars, shrines, and sacrifices, (21) as befits their nature—she that is earthly, of a lighter and a laxer sort; she that is heavenly, purer and holier in type. And you may well conjecture, it is the earthly goddess, the common Aphrodite, who sends forth the bodily loves; while from her that is named of heaven, Ourania, proceed those loves which feed upon the soul, on friendship and on noble deeds. It is by this latter, Callias, that you are held in bonds, if I mistake not, Love divine. (22) This I infer as well from the fair and noble character of your friend, as from the fact that you invite his father to share your life and intercourse. (23) Since no part of these is hidden from the father by the fair and noble lover.

*(19) For Aphrodite Ourania and Pandemos see Plat. "Symp." 180.*

*(20) Lit. "that is believed to be the same." See Cic. "De N. D." iii. 16. Cf. Aesch. "Prom." 210 (of Themis and Gaia), {pollon onomaton morphe mia}.*

*(21) e.g. to Aphrodite Pandemos a white goat, {mekas leuke}, but to Aphrodite Ourania a heifer, and {thusiai nephaliai}, offerings without wine, i.e. of water, milk, and honey. Schol. to Soph. "Oed. Col." 100; Lucian, lxvii. "Dial. Mer." 7. 1.*

*(22) Lit. "by Eros."*

*(23) Cf. Plat. "Prot." 318 A; Aristoph. "Thesmoph." 21, "learned*

*conversazioni."*

Hermogenes broke in: By Hera, Socrates, I much admire you for many things, and now to see how in the act of gratifying Callias you are training him in duty and true excellence. (24)

*(24) Lit. "teaching him what sort of man he ought to be." This, as we know, is the very heart and essence of the Socratic (= {XS}) method. See "Mem." I. ii. 3.*

Why, yes (he said), if only that his cup of happiness may overflow, I wish to testify to him how far the love of soul is better than the love of body.

Without friendship, (25) as we full well know, there is no society of any worth. And this friendship, what is it? On the part of those whose admiration (26) is bestowed upon the inner disposition, it is well named a sweet and voluntary compulsion. But among those whose desire (26) is for the body, there are not a few who blame, nay hate, the ways of their beloved ones. And even where attachment (26) clings to both, (27) even so the bloom of beauty after all does quickly reach its prime; the flower withers, and when that fails, the affection which was based upon it must also wither up and perish. But the soul, with every step she makes in her onward course towards deeper wisdom, grows ever worthier of love.

*(25) Lit. "That without love no intercourse is worth regarding, we all know."*

*(26) N.B.—{agamenon, epithumounton, sterxosi}. Here, as often, the author seems to have studied the {orthoepeia} of Prodicus. See "Mem." II. i. 24.*

*(27) i.e. "body and character."*

Ay, and in the enjoyment of external beauty a sort of surfeit is engendered. Just as the eater's appetite palls through repletion with regard to meats, (28) so will the feelings of a lover towards his idol. But the soul's attachment, owing to its purity, knows no satiety. (29) Yet not therefore, as a man might fondly deem, has it less of the character of loveliness. (30) But very clearly herein is our prayer fulfilled, in which we beg the goddess to grant us words and deeds that bear the impress of her own true loveliness. (31)

*(28) Cf. "Mem." III. xi. 13.*

*(29) Lit. "is more insatiate." Cf. Charles Wesley's hymn:*

O Love Divine, how sweet Thou art! When shall I find my willing heart All taken up by Thee?

*(30) Lit. "is she, the soul, more separate from Aphrodite."*

*(31) Or, "stamped with the image of Aphrodite." Zeune cf. Lucr. i. 24, addressing Venus, "te sociam studeo scribendis versibus esse," "I would have thee for a helpmate in writing the verses..."; and below, 28, "quo magis aeternum da dictis, diva, leporem," "Wherefore all the more, O lady, lend my lays an ever-living charm" (H. A. J. Munro).*

That a soul whose bloom is visible alike in beauty of external form, free and unfettered, and an inner disposition, bashful, generous; a spirit (32) at once imperial and affable, (33) born to rule among its fellows—that such a being will, of course, admire and fondly cling to his beloved, is a thesis which needs no further argument on my part. Rather I will essay to teach you, how it is natural that this same type of lover should in turn be loved by his soul's idol. (34)

*(32) Cf. Plat. "Phaedr." 252 E.*

*(33) The epithet {philophron} occurs "Mem." III. i. 6, of a general; ib. III. v. 3 (according to the vulg. reading), of the Athenians.*

*(34) Or, "the boy whom he cherishes."*

How, in the first place, is it possible for him to hate a lover who, he knows, regards him as both beautiful and good? (35) and, in the next place, one who, it is clear, is far more anxious to promote the fair estate of him he loves (36) than to indulge his selfish joys? and above all, when he has faith and trust that neither dereliction, (37) nor loss of beauty through sickness, nor aught else, will diminish their affection.

*(35) Or, "perfection."*

*(36) Lit. "the boy."*

*(37) Reading {en para ti poiese}. Al. "come what come may," lit. "no alteration"; or if reading {parebese} transl. "although his May of youth should pass, and sickness should mar his features, the tie of friendship will not be weakened."*

If, then, they own a mutual devotion, (38) how can it but be, they will take delight in gazing each into the other's eyes, hold kindly converse, trust and be trusted, have forethought for each other, in success rejoice together, in misfortune share their troubles; and so long as health endures make merry cheer, day in day out; or if either of them should fall on sickness, then will their intercourse be yet more constant; and if they cared for one another face to face, much more will they care when parted. (39) Are not all these the outward tokens of true loveliness? (40) In the exercise of such sweet offices, at any rate, they show their passion for holy friendship's state, and prove its bliss, continuously pacing life's path from youth to eld.

*(38) For beauty of style (in the original) Zeune cf. "Mem." II. vi. 28 foll.; III. xi. 10.*

*(39) "Albeit absent from one another in the body, they are more present in the soul." Cf. Virg. "Aen." iv. 83, "illum absens absentem auditque videtque."*

*(40) Or, "bear the stamp of Aphrodite."*

But the lover who depends upon the body, (41) what of him? First, why should love-for-love be given to such a lover? because, forsooth, he bestows upon himself what he desires, and upon his minion things of dire reproach? or that what he hastens to exact, infallibly must separate that other from his nearest friends?

*(41) Or, "is wholly taken up with." Cf. Plat. "Laws," 831 C.*

If it be pleaded that persuasion is his instrument, not violence; is that no reason rather for a deeper loathing? since he who uses violence (42) at any rate declares himself in his true colours as a villain, while the tempter corrupts the soul of him who yields to his persuasions.

*(42) Cf. "Hiero," iii. 3; "Cyrop." III. i. 39.*

Ay, and how should he who traffics with his beauty love the purchaser, any more than he who keeps a stall in the market-place and vends to the highest bidder? Love springs not up, I trow, because the one is in his prime, and the other's bloom is withered, because fair is mated with what is not fair, and hot lips are pressed to cold. Between man and woman it is different. There the wife at any rate shares with her husband in their nuptial joys; but here conversely, the one is sober and with unimpassioned eye regards his fellow, who is drunken with the wine of passion. (43)

*(43) Lit. "by Aphrodite." Cf. Plat. "Phaedr." 240, "But the lover*

*... when he is drunk" (Jowett); "Symp." 214 C.*

Wherefore it is no marvel if, beholding, there springs up in his breast the bitterest contempt and scorn for such a lover. Search and you shall find that nothing harsh was ever yet engendered by attachment based on moral qualities; whilst shameless intercourse, time out of mind, has been the source of countless hateful and unhallowed deeds. (44)

*(44) Zeune cf. Ael. "V. H." viii. 9, re Archelaus king of Macedon,*

*concerning whom Aristotle, "Pol." v. 10. 1311 B: "Many*

*conspiracies have originated in shameful attempts made by*

*sovereigns on the persons of their subjects. Such was the attack*

*of Crataeus upon Archelaus," etc. (Jowett).*

I have next to show that the society of him whose love is of the body, not the soul, is in itself illiberal. The true educator who trains another in the path of virtue, who will teach us excellence, whether of speech or conduct, (45) may well be honoured, even as Cheiron and Phoenix (46) were honoured by Achilles. But what can he expect, who stretches forth an eager hand to clutch the body, save to be treated (47) as a beggar? That is his character; for ever cringing and petitioning a kiss, or some other soft caress, (48) this sorry suitor dogs his victims.

*(45) Phoenix addresses Achilles, "Il." ix. 443:*

{muthon te reter' emenai, prektera te ergon}

Therefore sent he (Peleus) me to thee to teach thee all things, To be both a speaker of words and a doer of deeds (W. Leaf).

*(46) See "Il." xi. 831; "Hunting," ch. i., as to Cheiron and his*

*scholars, the last of whom is Achilles.*

*(47) {an periepoito}. "He will be scurvily treated." Cf. "Hell." III. i. 19.*

*(48) Cf. "Mem." I. ii. 29.*

If my language has a touch of turbulence, (49) do not marvel: partly the wine exalts me; partly that love which ever dwells within my heart of hearts now pricks me forward to use great boldness of speech (50) against his base antagonist. Why, yes indeed, it seems to me that he who fixes his mind on outward beauty is like a man who has taken a farm on a short lease. He shows no anxiety to improve its value; his sole object being to take off it the largest crops he can himself. But he whose heart is set on loyal friendship resembles rather a man who has a farmstead of his own. At any rate, he scours the wide world to find what may enhance the value of his soul's delight. (51)

*(49) Or, "wantonness"; and for the apology see Plat. "Phaedr." 238: "I appear to be in a divine fury, for already I am getting into dithyrambics" (Jowett).*

*(50) Lit. "to speak openly against that other sort of love which is its rival."*

*(51) Cf. Michelet, I think, as to the French peasant-farmer regarding his property as "sa femme."*

Again, let us consider the effect upon the object of attachment. Let him but know his beauty is a bond sufficient to enthrall his lover, (52) and what wonder if he be careless of all else and play the wanton. Let him discover, on the contrary, that if he would retain his dear affection he must himself be truly good and beautiful, and it is only natural he should become more studious of virtue. But the greatest blessing which descends on one beset with eager longing to convert the idol of his soul into a good man and true friend is this: necessity is laid upon himself to practise virtue; since how can he hope to make his comrade good, if he himself works wickedness? Is it conceivable that the example he himself presents of what is shameless and incontinent, (53) will serve to make the beloved one temperate and modest?

*(52) Or, "that by largess of beauty he can enthrall his lover."*

*(53) See Plat. "Symp." 182 A, 192 A.*

I have a longing, Callias, by mythic argument (54) to show you that not men only, but gods and heroes, set greater store by friendship of the soul than bodily enjoyment. Thus those fair women (55) whom Zeus, enamoured of their outward beauty, wedded, he permitted mortal to remain; but those heroes whose souls he held in admiration, these he raised to immortality. Of whom are Heracles and the Dioscuri, and there are others also named. (56) As I maintain, it was not for his body's sake, but for his soul's, that Ganymede (57) was translated to Olympus, as the story goes, by Zeus. And to this his very name bears witness, for is it not written in Homer?

*And he gladdens ({ganutai}) to hear his voice. (58)*

This the poet says, meaning "he is pleased to listen to his words."

*(54) Or, "I have a desire to romance a little," "for your benefit to*
*explain by legendary lore." Cf. Isocr. 120 C; Plat. "Rep." 392 B.*

*(55) e.g. Leda, Danae, Europa, Alcmena, Electra, Latona, Laodamia*
*(Zeune).*

*(56) See "Hunting," i.; "Hell." VI. iii. 6.*

*(57) See Plat. "Phaedr." 255 C; Cic. "Tusc." i. 26, "nec Homerum audio*
*... divina mallem ad nos," a protest against anthropomorphism in*
*religion.*

*(58) Not in "our" version of Homer, but cf. "Il." xx. 405, {ganutai de*
*te tois 'Enosikhthon}; "Il." xiii. 493, {ganutai d' ara te phrena*
*poimen}.*

And again, in another passage he says:

*Knowing deep devices ({medea}) in his mind, (59)*

which is as much as to say, "knowing wise counsels in his mind." Ganymede, therefore, bears a name compounded of the two words, "joy" and "counsel," and is honoured among the gods, not as one "whose body," but "whose mind" "gives pleasure."

*(59) Partly "Il." xxiv. 674, {pukina phresi mede' ekhontes}; and "Il." xxiv. 424, {phila phresi medea eidos}. Cf. "Od." vi. 192; xviii. 67, 87; xxii. 476.*

Furthermore (I appeal to you, Niceratus), (60) Homer makes Achilles avenge Patroclus in that brilliant fashion, not as his favourite, but as his comrade. (61) Yes, and Orestes and Pylades, (62) Theseus and Peirithous, (63) with many another noble pair of demigods, are celebrated as having wrought in common great and noble deeds, not because they lay inarmed, but because of the admiration they felt for one another.

*(60) As an authority on Homer.*

*(61) Cf. Plat. "Symp." 179 E: "The notion that Patroclus was the beloved one is a foolish error into which Aeschylus has fallen," etc. (in his "Myrmidons"). See J. A. Symonds, "The Greek Poets," 2nd series, "Achilles," p. 66 foll.*

*(62) Concerning whom Ovid ("Pont." iii. 2. 70) says, "nomina fama tenet."*

*(63) See Plut. "Thes." 30 foll. (Clough, i. p. 30 foll.); cf. Lucian, xli. "Toxaris," 10.*

Nay, take the fair deeds of to-day: and you shall find them wrought rather for the sake of praise by volunteers in toil and peril, than by men accustomed to choose pleasure in place of honour. And yet Pausanias, (64) the lover of the poet Agathon, (65) making a defence in behalf (66) of some who wallow in incontinence, has stated that an army composed of lovers and beloved would be invincible. (67) These, in his opinion, would, from awe of one another, have the greatest horror of destruction. A truly marvellous argument, if he means that men accustomed to turn deaf ears to censure and to behave to one another shamelessly, are more likely to feel ashamed of doing a shameful deed. He adduced as evidence the fact that the Thebans and the Eleians (68) recognise the very principle, and added: Though they sleep inarmed, they do not scruple to range the lover side by side with the beloved one in the field of battle. An instance which I take to be no instance, or at any rate one-sided, (69) seeing that what they look upon as lawful with us is scandalous. (70) Indeed, it strikes me that this vaunted battle-order would seem to argue some mistrust on their part who adopt it—a suspicion that their bosom friends, once separated from them, may forget to behave as brave men should. But the men of Lacedaemon, holding that "if a man but lay his hand upon the body and for lustful purpose, he shall thereby forfeit claim to what is beautiful and noble"—do, in the spirit of their creed, contrive to mould and fashion their "beloved ones" to such height of virtue, (71) that should these find themselves drawn up with foreigners, albeit no longer side by side with their own lovers, (72) conscience will make desertion of their present friends impossible. Self-respect constrains them: since the goddess whom the men of Lacedaemon worship is not "Shamelessness," but "Reverence." (73)

*(64) See Cobet, "Pros. Xen." p. 15; Plat. "Protag." 315 D; Ael. "V. H." ii. 21.*

*(65) Ib.; Aristot. "Poet." ix.*

*(66) Or, "in his 'Apology' for."*

*(67) Plat. "Symp." 179 E, puts the sentiment into the mouth of Phaedrus: "And if there were only some way of contriving that a state or an army should be made up of lovers and their loves, they would be the very best governors of their own city, abstaining from all dishonour, and emulating one another in honour; and when fighting at one another's side, although not a mere handful, they would overcome the world. For what lover would not choose rather to be seen by all mankind than by his beloved, either when abandoning his post or throwing away his arms? He would be ready*

*to die a thousand deaths rather than endure this. Or would desert his beloved or fail him in the hour of danger? The veriest coward would become an inspired hero, equal to the bravest, at such a time; Love would inspire him. That courage which, as Homer says, the god breathes into the soul of heroes, Love of his own nature infuses into the lover" (Jowett). Cf. "Hunting," xii. 20; "Anab." VII. iv. 7; "Cyrop." VII. i. 30.*

(68) Sc. in their institutions. Cf. Plat. "Symp." 182, "in Elis and Boeotia"; "Pol. Lac." ii. 13; Ael. "V. H." iii. 12, xiii. 5; Athen. xiii. 2. For the Theban Sacred Band see Plut. "Pelop." 18, 19 (Clough, ii. 218).

(69) Or, "not in pari materia, so to speak."

(70) Is not Xenophon imputing himself to Socrates? Henkel cf. Plat. "Crito," 52 E. See Newman, op. cit. i. 396.

(71) Or, "shape to so fine a manhood that..."

(72) Reading {en te aute taxei}. Al. {... polei}, transl. "nor indeed in the same city." Cf. "Hell." V. iv. 33, re death of Cleonymus at Leuctra.

(73) Lit. "Aidos not Anaideia." See Paus. "Lac." xx. 10; "Attica," xvii. 1; Cic. "de Leg." ii. 11, a reference which I owe to M. Eugene Talbot, "Xen." i. 236.

I fancy we should all agree with one another on the point in question, if we thus approached it. Ask yourself to which type of the two must he (74) accord, to whom you would entrust a sum of money, make him the

- 63 -

guardian of your children, look to find in him a safe and sure depositary of any favour? (75) For my part, I am certain that the very lover addicted to external beauty would himself far sooner have his precious things entrusted to the keeping of one who has the inward beauty of the soul. (76)

*(74) He (the master-mistress of my passion).*

*(75) {kharitas} = "kindly offices," beneficia. Cf. "Ages." iv. 4;*

*"Mem." IV. iv. 17. Al. = delicias, "to deposit some darling*

*object."*

*(76) Or, "some one truly lovable in soul and heart."*

Ah, yes! and you, my friend (he turned to Callias), you have good reason to be thankful to the gods who of their grace inspired you with love for your Autolycus. Covetous of honour, (77) beyond all controversy, must he be, who could endure so many toils and pains to hear his name proclaimed (78) victor in the "pankration."

*(77) See "Mem." II. iii. 16; "Isocr." 189 C, {ph. kai megalopsukhoi}.*

*(78) i.e. "by the public herald."*

But what if the thought arose within him: (79) his it is not merely to add lustre to himself and to his father, but that he has ability, through help of manly virtue, to benefit his friends and to exalt his fatherland, by trophies which he will set up against our enemies in war, (80) whereby he will himself become the admired of all observers, nay, a name to be remembered among Hellenes and barbarians. (81) Would he not in that case, think you, make much of (82) one whom he regarded as his bravest fellow-worker, laying at his feet the greatest honours?

*(79) Cf. Theogn. 947:*

{patrida kosmeso, liparen polin, out' epi demo trepsas out' adikois andrasi peithomenos}.

*(80) Who in 421 B.C. were of course the Lacedaemonians and the allies.*

*Autolycus was killed eventually by the Thirty to please the*

*Lacedaemonian harmost. See Plut. "Lysand." 15 (Clough, iii. 120);*

*Paus. i. 18. 3; ix. 32. 8. Cf. "Hell." II. iii. 14.*

*(81) Cf. "Anab." IV. i. 20; "Mem." III. vi. 2.*

*(82) {periepein}. Cf. "Cyrop." IV. iv. 12; "Mem." II. ix. 5.*

If, then, you wish to be well-pleasing in his eyes, you had best inquire by what knowledge Themistocles (83) was able to set Hellas free. You should ask yourself, what keen wit belonged to Pericles (83) that he was held to be the best adviser of his fatherland. You should scan (84) the field of history to learn by what sage wisdom Solon (85) established for our city her consummate laws. I would have you find the clue to that peculiar training by which the men of Lacedaemon have come to be regarded as the best of leaders. (86) Is it not at your house that their noblest citizens are lodged as representatives of a foreign state? (87)

*(83) See "Mem." II. vi. 13; III. vi. 2; IV. ii. 2.*

*(84) For the diction, {skepteon, skepteon, aphreteon, ereuneteon, epistamenos, eidos, philosopheras}, Xenophon's rhetorical style imitates the {orthoepeia} of Prodicus.*

*(85) See "Econ." xiv. 4.*

*(86) Or, "won for themselves at all hands the reputation of noblest generalship." Cf. "Ages." i. 3; "Pol. Lac." xiv. 3.*

*(87) Reading as vulg. {proxenoi d' ei...} or if with Schenkl, {proxenos d' ei...} transl. "You are their consul-general; at your house their noblest citizens are lodged from time to time." As to the office, cf. Dem. 475. 10; 1237. 17; Thuc. ii. 29; Boeckh, "P. E. A." 50. Callias appears as the Lac. {proxenos} ("Hell." V. iv. 22) 378 B.C., and at Sparta, 371 B.C., as the peace commissioner ("Hell." VI. iii. 3).*

Be sure that our state of Athens would speedily entrust herself to your direction were you willing. (88) Everything is in your favour. You are of noble family, "eupatrid" by descent, a priest of the divinities, (89) and of Erechtheus' famous line, (90) which with Iacchus marched to encounter the barbarian. (91) And still, at the sacred festival to-day, it is agreed that no one among your ancestors has ever been more fitted to discharge the priestly office than yourself; yours a person the goodliest to behold in all our city, and a frame adapted to undergo great toils.

*(88) Cf. "Mem." III. vii.*

*(89) i.e. Demeter and Core. Callias (see "Hell." VI. l.c.) was dadouchos (or torch-holder) in the mysteries.*

*(90) Or, "whose rites date back to Erechtheus." Cf. Plat. "Theag." 122.*

*(91) At Salamis. The tale is told by Herod. viii. 65, and Plut. "Themist." 15; cf. Polyaen. "Strat." iii. 11. 2. Just as Themistocles had won the battle of Salamis by help of Iacchus on the 16th Boedromion, the first day of the mysteries, so Chabrias won the sea-fight of Naxos by help of the day itself, {to 'Alade mustai}, 376 B.C.*

But if I seem to any of you to indulge a vein more serious than befits the wine-cup, marvel not. It has long been my wont to share our city's passion for noble-natured souls, alert and emulous in pursuit of virtue.

He ended, and, while the others continued to discuss the theme of his discourse, Autolycus sat regarding Callias. That other, glancing the while at the beloved one, turned to Socrates.

Call. Then, Socrates, be pleased, as go-between, (92) to introduce me to the state, that I may employ myself in state affairs and never lapse from her good graces. (93)

*(92) Lit. "as pander."*

(93) So Critobulus in the conversation so often referred to. "Mem." II. vi.

Never fear (he answered), if only people see your loyalty to virtue is genuine, (94) not of mere repute. A false renown indeed is quickly seen for what it is worth, being tested; but true courage (95) (save only what some god hinder) perpetually amidst the storm and stress of circumstance (96) pours forth a brighter glory.

(94) See "Mem." I. vii. 1, passim; II. vi. 39; "Econ." x. 9.

(95) Cf. Thuc. ii. 42, {andragathia}, "true courage in the public service covers a multitude of private shortcomings."

(96) {en tais praxesi}. Cf. Plat. "Phaedr." 271 D, "in actual life."

## IX

On such a note he ended his discourse.

At that, Autolycus, whose hour for walking exercise had now come, arose. His father, Lycon, was about to leave the room along with him, but before so doing, turned to Socrates, remarking:

By Hera, Socrates, if ever any one deserved the appellation "beautiful and good," (1) you are that man!

(1) For {kalos ge kalathos} see "Econ." vii. 2 and passim.

So the pair departed. After they were gone, a sort of throne was first erected in the inner room abutting on the supper chamber. Then the Syracusan entered, with a speech:

With your good pleasure, sirs, Ariadne is about to enter the bridal chamber set apart for her and Dionysus. Anon Dionysus will appear, fresh from the table of the gods, wine-flushed, and enter to his bride. In the last scene the two will play (2) with one another.

(2) {paixountai}. The Syracusan naturally uses the Doric form. See Cobet, "Pros. Xen." p. 16, note 23. Rutherford, "N. Phrynicus," p. 91.

He had scarce concluded, when Ariadne entered, attired like a bride. She crossed the stage and sate herself upon the throne. Meanwhile, before the god himself appeared a sound of flutes was heard; the cadence of the Bacchic air proclaimed his coming.

At this point the company broke forth in admiration of the ballet-master. For no sooner did the sound of music strike upon the ear of Ariadne than something in her action revealed to all the pleasure which it caused her. She did not step forward to meet her lover, she did not rise even from her seat; but the flutter of her unrest was plain to see. (3)

*(3) Lit. "the difficulty she had to keep so still was evident."*

When Dionysus presently caught sight of her he loved, lightly he danced towards her, and with show of tenderest passion gently reclined upon her knees; his arms entwined about her lovingly, and upon her lips he sealed a kiss; (4)—she the while with most sweet bashfulness was fain to wind responsive arms about her lover; till the banqueters, the while they gazed all eyes, clapped hands and cried "Encore!" But when Dionysus rose upon his feet, and rising lifted Ariadne to her full height, the action of those lovers as they kissed and fondled one another was a thing to contemplate. (5) As to the spectators, they could see that Dionysus was indeed most beautiful, and Ariadne like some lovely blossom; nor were those mocking gestures, but real kisses sealed on loving lips; and so, (6) with hearts aflame, they gazed expectantly. They could hear the question asked by Dionysus, did she love him? and her answer, as prettily she swore she did. And withal so earnestly, not Dionysus only, but all present, had sworn an oath in common: the boy and girl were verily and indeed a pair of happy lovers. So much less did they resemble actors, trained to certain gestures, than two beings bent on doing what for many a long day they had set their hearts on.

*(4) Or, "and encircling his arms about her impressed upon her lips a kiss."*

*(5) Or, "then was it possible to see the more than mimic gestures."*
*(6) Or, "on the tiptoe of excitement." Cf. "Hell." III. i. 14, iv. 2.*

At last when these two lovers, caught in each other's arms, were seen to be retiring to the nuptial couch, the members of the supper party turned to withdraw themselves; and whilst those of them who were unmarried swore that they would wed, those who were wedded mounted their horses and galloped off to join their wives, in quest of married joys.

Only Socrates, and of the rest the few who still remained behind, anon set off with Callias, to see out Lycon and his son, and share the walk.

And so this supper party, assembled in honour of Autolycus, broke up.